Quests beyond Existence

by

Michael Duque

Dedicated to

GLENDA
HELINA MICHAELLA
CHRISTOPER GLENN
MARK GABRIEL

and

THE FAMILIES AND SPIRITS OF LOVED ONES
IN THESE QUESTS

ACKNOWLEDGEMENTS AND WITH THANKS:

My wife Glenda for her untiring support;

My lovely children for their unending inspiration;

Tony Perez for awakening the writer in me;

The Spirit Questors, particularly Chiqui Martinez, Ian Opena,
Sheila Medallon, Chi De Jesus, Connie Allones, Jing Opena,
Tina Tayag, Elo Rebollido, Don Reyes, Neil Engracia,
Sharlene Benedicto, Marlon Lacsamana, and all the other
questors who have continuously gone out of their own
personal lives to help enrich and show unconditional
love amidst a world of materialism and conditions;

Emmanuel Reyes, my childhood friend, for helping
lay the foundation of all that is now;

My editor Ralph and creative director Filipo for their
untiring support and input to make this work extremely profound;

The people the questors call AGENTS, for allowing me to share our
experiences so that others may learn to love and live fruitfully;

The Beings not of this plane of existence for guiding me;

Finally, to the Great Architect of the Universe,
for my existence.

The Spirit Questors® is a group of young, psychic volunteers, who communicate with human and non-human entities in the service of peaceful co-existence and unconditional love.

 Primarily, the Spirit Questors exist as a responsible forum where students of New Age, psychics, adepts and the uninitiated can exchange and interact key concepts about the paranormal, occult and the New Age.

The Questors also provide information that will help serve up for the physical, social and spiritual educational needs of the society. Furthermore, the group acts as a resource for further learning, growth and understanding.

* *

The Spirit Questors envision to build and realize a society of **peaceful co-existence** based on the positive interaction and the healing of spirits, elementals and people through the active practice of **unconditional love**.

The Spirit Questors enliven this vision by:
- Respecting the Freewill of each individual
- Aiming to be truthful and honest in all endeavours
- Avoiding depriving any being of their right to exist
- Using psychism and other paranormal resources in a responsible manner
- Employing and exhausting all possible means of negotiating and compromise in dealings involving spirits, elementals and beings of the higher realm
- Avoiding any acts that banish and evict
- Working together without prejudice of education, social status, religion, belief and personal background

PRIMARY PURPOSE
The Spirit Questors envision peaceful co-existence based on the healing of and positive interaction with people, the spirits of the deceased, elementals and higher beings through the practice of unconditional love.

SECONDARY PURPOSE

1. Respect the free will of each individual.
2. Strive to be truthful in all endeavours.
3. Avoid depriving any being of their right to exist.
4. Exist as a responsible forum where students of New Age, Psychics and Adept and the uninitiated can dialogue on key concepts that will help provide for physical, social, and spiritual education of the society.

www.spiritquestors.com
www.spiritquestors.org
Email: requests@spiritquestors.com
Tel: +63.915.4630540

Table of Contents

Spirit Questors ···························· vii

Introduction ···························· 3

The Beginning ···························· 5

Informal Training ···························· 8

Transformation ···························· 10

Cheliog ···························· 17

A Love Like No Other ···························· 26

Ilocos ···························· 36

Dance of light ···························· 58

Astral Drive ···························· 76

Deva ···························· 103

Maiden, Mother and Crone ···························· 122

The Greatest Love of All ···························· 134

Dolor ···························· 146

Tree Dwellers ···························· 160

The Guardian ···························· 176

Introduction

The sun has set. Darkness is almost everywhere, except for the multi-coloured neon billboard across the street. It is already half-ten at night. Total darkness is around me. Alone in a place known for its unexplained nightly occurrences, the experience is unnerving, if not totally frightening.

As I sat, crossed-leg, in the centre of the second-floor hallway of this previously prominent female boarding school which has now become a bustling university, an unusual sensation filled my body.

Perplexed and curious, I started to shiver in cold. My arms started getting eerily cold. I was starting to strain my eyes in the complete blackness around me when a sudden surge of extremely cold air snapped me back to my consciousness.

I could now vaguely discern a darker than dark figure emerge from my right. I simultaneously felt love and consolation to a certain degree. I closed my eyes, hoping that the vision will disappear. It does not.

After some time, the figure started moving slowly to my left. The words "Do not be afraid," and "I come in peace," repeatedly flashed inside my mind.

The thoughts are not mine, however, for I am too pre-occupied with what I am seeing physically. "Who are you?" I asked, consciously, and to my surprise, the letters Y-A-T-A-N began repeating itself in sequence.

"Tanya?" I asked blankly. Immediately, the letters disappeared and vanished.

Silence. Then I said, "I also come here in peace. My name is…" after which, I sensed a smile from somewhere.

"I work with the university's publication as one of its editors. I am here on a late night work. I just wanted to cool-off, had a heated argument with my editor-in-chief," I mentally said.

Again, I sensed a smile.

Tanya is a young woman in her early twenties. She's about 5 feet, 6 inches tall, with a long, dark silky hair and a very pale complexion. It seemed that she knew what had happened and appreciated my sense of understanding.

"I believe in you," she said. Furthermore, Tanya said that she has been watching me on campus since my first year.

A beam of light suddenly flashed from nowhere. I heard familiar voices. Quickly, I mentally said, "It is a pleasure to meet you. I must go. Please feel free to visit me anytime at the editorial office at the ground level of this building. Thanks."

At that point, 3 familiar figures coming from the hallways' blind corner appeared on my right.

With a torch in hand and snuggled close together in obvious fear, my colleagues Darlyl, Haidee and Aurora have come looking for me. They asked me to forget about the incident in the office earlier. I teasingly smiled at them before agreeing to call it a night.

Walking down to the lobby, I glanced at the hallway once again. I thought about my unusual experience, and the new "friend" I had just met. As we walked past the university gates, a happy thought swelled inside me. I knew deep down that I would be seeing Tanya again.

I found comfort knowing that somebody will be watching over me in campus. A special friend I found, indeed.

NOTE:

All names and identifying characteristics of those involved in these stories have been changed or altered accordingly to protect their privacy and identity. However, the essence of the stories and the non-human aspects remain as profound and as factual as possible.

The Beginning

I was five-years old when I first had my experience in human spirits. It was 1977, Christmas time, the whole clan had gathered for the annual reunion in our family holiday apartment.

I was watching our nanny help my youngest brother get dressed when he started giggling all of a sudden while pointing at the door. Somebody else was entertaining my brother, but it was neither me nor our nanny.

With our backs turned towards the door, my nanny and I looked behind us. Instantaneously, she screamed as we both saw my Granddad smiling back at us. My nanny fainted, and the next thing I remember is my aunt carrying me out of the room to the foyer where everybody else was.

It was then that I remembered that my Granddad, my mother's father, had died exactly 3 months earlier!

I don't have fond memories of my maternal grandfather, partially because I grew up with my paternal grandparents, but I will always remember that single occasion with vividness and clarity more than any other childhood experiences I have had. And that's because starting that day, numerous other unnatural occurrences have since happened to me.

Growing up, I was taught that every living thing deserves love and respect. A total harmony among all living creatures should exist. Social status, financial or physical constraints are not to be taken as hindrances in giving each creature equal love, care and respect. All beings are equal. I soon came to understand that sin is a state of self-guilt and harm, be it physical, emotional, moral or spiritual. I further explored my surroundings and tried to find answers to my early idealism.

Fright night on campus

Way back in 1970's, when I was still in grade school, I participated in an overnight camping event in campus that gave me another unexpected experience in human spirits.

Our primary school building is situated in the east in the innermost part of the huge campus. The building stood 6-storeys high, facing the secondary level building. Together, they formed an "**L**" shape. The open quadrangle provided strategic views of both the building's corridors and its facade.

While we were about to ascend a flight of stairs, a flash of faint white silhouette suddenly caught our eyes. Instinctively they followed the ethereal shadow while I retreated to the quadrangle in front of the 2 buildings.

From my vantage point, I can see the lead group at the 4th floor corridor to the north. But from the corner of my eye, however, I could see a faint ethereal shadow on the southern side going to the sixth floor. I refocused my torch on the vision but it disappeared.

By the time our search group reached the southern side of the building's fifth floor, the faint white ghostly glow appeared again, this time on the north side of the building's sixth floor. It is, however, not as faint as it first appeared. The figure is now much brighter and is clearly visible.

As if on cue, it turned to a corner away from my sight, and a disturbing thought of "goodbye" kept running through my mind.

The sightings which took place kept repeating itself inside my head and it disturbed me. I was deep in thought trying to find the reason behind that experience. I just could not let this thing pass without any explanation.

As I was searching for my answer, I heard a very disturbing sound. I tried to locate where the sound may have come from but I just couldn't. And this time, I got really scared.

Creepy underneath the blanket

Tic-tac-tic-tac. "I want to learn to type," I said to my mom.

"You can continue tomorrow, it's almost midnight," my mother frowned.

I wanted to continue learning and practicing my typing skills but mom said no, so I had to quit. Exhausted, I set aside the old manual typewriter, switched the room lights off, and went to my sleeping quarters. A few minutes later, the typewriter started clicking on its own.

In the darkness, my mom yelled, "Did I not tell you to stop and go to sleep?"

"But mom, it's not me," I protested.

Tic-tac-tic-tac. The typing went on for another 5-minutes, and then it eventually stopped. The room was again covered in darkness and silence.

As I lay in bed with the blanket covering over me, I remained fully awake, still conscious and very sensitive to my surroundings.

At this state, I felt my legs getting colder than before. The coldness crept towards my arms, neck and head. The sensation is starting to overwhelm me. The cold is now from inside. I am starting to have goose bumps. My ears feel extremely cold.

Underneath the blanket, something unnatural is happening. Once more, I knew that I was experiencing something that defies logic and explanation.

Informal Training

I joined the Air Force reserve officers training corps in college. But as a consequence, I also had to end, quite hesitantly, my promising career as a member of the school's soccer varsity team. While in training, Emmanuel and I became friends. At that time, he is already into psychology and the paranormal.

Once during my visit to their humble abode, he asked me if I would be interested in Psychology.

"Try me," I shot back.

That conversation started a deeper friendship between us as we both found a fascination in Applied Psychology. His dad and younger brother were more into the paranormal.

During one of our practical exercises, I remember having undergone a series of mental processes where you need to do the following:

"Relax. Slowly breathe in...breath out. Now, continue relaxing while you think of nothing. Do not think of anything. Let everything come naturally."

Then it ends with how it began. "Relax. Slowly breathe in...breath out."

Generally, this is called meditation, or the process of attuning oneself to the higher vibrations of nature.

Meditation supplements an individual's awareness of the self. Prayer, in itself, is a form of meditation. Meditation is common to all forms of cultural diversity. It is a form of relaxation technique both physical and spiritual. It is best done at least once a day for about 15-20 minutes. It is also a form of stress management.

With meditation as the foundation for my search of inner knowledge, I am able to quickly attune and centre myself. Its awakening effects greatly enhance the study of the occult and mysticism. It opens up a new level of sensitivity and consciousness.

Practiced in various ways, the end-point of all meditations will always be the same – the awakening of oneself to a higher level of consciousness.

Many great individuals have practiced meditation in one way or another. Gautama Buddha in his search for enlightenment, and Jesus in his intense moments of prayers, have all practiced meditation to its fullest.

Emmanuel has effectively guided me through meditation until I became confident of doing it by myself. Today, whenever time and circumstances permit, I make it a point to practice meditation daily.

Transformation

The sun is awfully hot and dry. A summer holiday is in the offing, so my college friends and I decided to visit south of the archipelago.

Along the way, sceneries of vast farmlands and the majestic Mayon Volcano make me wonder who made all these possible – ahh, such is the power of the greatest author of this novel called life.

Perfectly sitting amidst Mayon Volcano's now imperfect cone is a halo-like circle of clouds. The horizon continues to inspire and create artists among those who continue to ponder on its majestic beauty.

It was to be my very first visit in the region and it really excited me. The vast greenery and expansive landscapes of rice and corn crops has stuck me with awe and speculation – and it continues to haunt me until today.

In hindsight, the simplicity of rural life also made me think of all the wonderful things that city life can offer. The comforts and the luxury of the acropolis have somehow been the cause of mass pilgrims into the city.

We stayed in Emerita's place first before heading for the house of Delia's aunt, which entails a long two-hour trek through mountain-side terrains and rice paddies. The walk begins after a bumpy, two-hour jeepney ride from Emerita's place to the quintessential town of Nabua.

As we walked, the summer sun shone its late afternoon rays in the golden sea of "palay" (rice), swaying and dancing with the shrewd blowing of the gentle breeze. The almost ripe rice grains displayed an orchestrated movement of exceptional beauty. In the meantime, the river gave a passionate touch to the scenery -- like blood giving life to each and every living creature.

The river is dry at this time of the year making our cross so much easier. A short walk down the trail that cuts through the edge of the mountain jungle eventually brought us to an entirely new setting. It is as if we had just stepped through another time zone. As far as our eyes can see, there is nary a trace of any form of civilization or the comforts of city life. We are in the middle of nowhere.

Finally hidden beneath the tall and huge acacia trees and firmly protected on the west and north sides by the fatherly slopes of the mountain where it cradles, is a simple grass gazebo called *bahay-kubo*.

Delia's aunt lives in this hut. Made of inter-twined coconut leaves and bamboo shoots, her hut faces wide expansive rice fields just before the dried-up river.

We hurriedly settled in for a late afternoon snack of root crops and tea made of boiled leaves. Sitting on a tree stump, I witnessed the sun's golden rays falter and turn orange before slowly disappearing in the horizon. Darkness will soon become inevitable, I told myself.

Indeed, just after a few minutes, pitch black was soon everywhere.

At this time, the moon has not shown itself yet and the sound of nature's life was further amplified by the deafening silence. A hearty dinner of boiled native chicken graciously served with steamed rice satisfied our tired and weary bodies from the long journey before now.

After dinner, we all settled in for a good night's sleep. Being in a *bahay-kubo*, we laid dried grass mats called *"banig"* on the bamboo floor as our makeshift beds. I laid my mat near the door while Emerita and all the other girls clustered together at the far end of the room. Our only source of light is a gas-filled lamp that burned dimly behind the walled grass partition.

At about half-past ten, I noticed Emerita getting very uneasy and anxious. Knowing her to be a sound sleeper and a highly intuitive person, I asked her what was wrong. By this time, everybody was awake. Likewise, everyone was wondering what is wrong with her.

"How are you feeling?" I asked her.

Almost hysterical, she replied, "I don't know. I have this very funny sensation, almost panicky."

"Panicky with what," I clarified.

"I don't know," she mumbled, while continuing to appear tense and agitated.

Although puzzled at her reaction and behaviour, I reassured her that everything will be fine. I myself acted nonchalantly but deep inside, I knew something is amiss and it bothered me.

I had this unmistakable feeling of wanting to go out of the house for some reason. When I told Delia that I wanted to go out of the house, she protested strongly and persuaded me to stay. Not wanting to be disrespectful, I decided to just pre-occupy myself with some form of meditation.

I sat crossed-leg by the door, straightened my spine and adjusted my weight until I was comfortable. I laid my hands on my lap and started breathing in and out slowly at first until I was able to control my breathing.

Relying on my memory of the hut and its immediate surroundings, I envisioned the whole place again inside my mind. In my mind's eye, I then slowly walked around the area. As I did the mental exercise, I sensed three shadowy figures alongside me.

The figures are not clearly visible but I had a feeling that they were dishevelled and untidy. I also sensed that they are floating in the air. It puzzled me no end as I could not see any form of wings on them.

Their hairs, long enough to slide past their shoulders, were in total disarray. As they moved quickly from one place to another, I could hear a very faint but distinct sound of air movement.

I then opened my eyes. Not wanting to scare the group with what I thought I just saw, I asked everybody to relax and keep still. I then reassumed my meditation position.

Deep inside, I simply wanted to reconfirm if I will be able to get the same thoughts or visions.

After a few minutes, I eventually got the same vision of 3 distinct floating figures. This time however, one of the figures is now just outside the door where I was and the other 2 were on the roof.

I wanted to physically rush outside the house and confront these 3 shadowy figures yet something inside myself was preventing me from doing so.

Suddenly I became aware of instinctively forming a blue ball of light, much like a bubble, around me.

I expanded the bubble to those around me and eventually, I saw the vision of a huge blue bubble around the hut.

I kept my focus on the bubble for sometime. Then I felt relaxed and satisfied. Slowly, I opened my eyes.

Turning to Emerita, I then asked her, "So how do you feel now?"

"I feel so much better. What did you just do?" she shot back.

"Nothing," I said, "You can go back to sleep now." With that, I felt relieved, feeling happy with the situation and at peace with myself.

Waking up the following day, I recounted the events of the previous night and its surrounding mysteries. I asked everyone for an explaination but no one can give me a straight answer.

Tower of light

In the mid-1990's, a few days prior to Christmas, I found myself in front of a big bookstore in one of the large malls in Manila looking for a gift for Emmanuel.

Knowing his passion for books, I wanted to give him an interesting book for the season. I strolled around the place, browsing for books that were on sale and leafing through the pages of any unusual book I saw.

"No Private Reading"

This was clearly posted around the place in big bold red letters, but I took no heed of it. Most of the books were sealed in a protective, transparent cover, except for one which served as a browsing copy.

As I scanned through the shelves, I came across a shiny little black book with a little red circle on a silver horizon. On its cover, printed in silver letters, read, "The Calling".

Instinctively, I reached for a copy and started to browse through it. Time passed quickly, and I wouldn't have noticed it had my legs not began to ache. By then, I was almost done reading the book's first chapter.

Then I recalled what I've just read:

"Relax. Relax your whole body. Now, imagine a shining blue ball of light one foot above your head. Visualize further this ball of light to being connected to the heavens, to a Divine Being, by a ray of light. Now, this ball of light becomes an extension of the Divine Being and from that same blue ball of light above your head, you'd slowly feel being bathed by light from that ball. Your head, shoulders, body and your legs would slowly become encapsulated by this ball of light. By this time, your whole being is enclosed by an aegis of light from the ball of light above your head. This protective light becomes your psychic shield that will protect you from unwanted energies. Should you

feel threatened, just visualize your psychic shield to protect you."

This entire process of meditation is called the Tower of Light.

There are variations of the tower of light, but the idea and objective are the same. Having read the tower of light in "The Calling," I got confused. A year ago, a similar process happened to me exactly as the book described.

I was able to finish reading the book sooner than I've expected.

After that incident, the experiences of spirit questors bothered me for some time but it also made good sense to me since I also began to understand my own personal experience. I strongly felt that their experiences, as well as that of mine, were just a part and parcel of a bigger set of experiences. Finally, I decided to write the following letter to Tony Perez of the Spirit Questors:

Dear Tony,

Greetings! I have long been compelled to write but have prevented myself from doing just so because for fear of criticism and rejection. I recently found the courage to do so.

I have quite followed publicized reports or material regarding you and your spirit questors. Frankly, I am quite interested into it, to a deeper level or understanding. But more than that interest, I feel as if I am compelled to be with it. Immediately after reading The Calling, the thought of either subduing the gift or developing it has long bothered me.

Since my childhood days, my family and I have experienced quite a number of such unnatural occurrences. This involves visions of past relatives, actual unexplained activities and the likes. In due time, these all temporarily ended. However, a friend re-introduced me into it.

Actually, my friend introduced me to the science of Psychology. Yet time urged me more into the Paranormal and the occult. I must admit that I did not put much effort into delving deeper.

I shelved the thought as time went by and as I became busy with school. Still, my unnatural occurrences continued. Experiences which I somehow can not quite piece together. Experiences that include visual sightings of entities, mental communication with various forms of entities, profound interest in shamanism, the occult, meditation and the likes.

I am even surprised that while reading your book, specifically about the blue protective light, I remembered to have actually done it a few months before, all without having known of the process. It all came naturally to me at that time.

My years of experiences have somewhat bothered me to an extent. Yet I am quite touch and bothered by your challenge. Yes, I do have a lot of questions in my mind but, am I to let them pass without an answer?

I do not think so. It is with this that I would like to ask your help and guidance in seeking out the answers to my questions and clarifying out my fears. I would also be very grateful if you will help me realize if what I have is a gift indeed or just a product of my imagination. If understanding and knowing would entail my selfless service or participation, so be it.

I hope I have not taken much of your time.

Thank you very much for bringing out the positive views in me. I also hope that this will be the start of a new beginning for me.

Again, thank you and God Bless.

Sincerely yours,
Michael

Cheliog

"Imagine a gold ball of light one foot above your head. Now, imagine a golden ray of light from the heavens connecting with the golden ball of light above your head. Then, starting from this golden ball of light, try picturing a ray of light slowly covering your whole body. This will be your psychic shield."

Thus said Buddy as he facilitated the Tower of Light and the Transformation of Fear exercises in front of the 2-storey house of Mrs. J. Wong, our agent.

A young and impeccable looking man of a few words, Buddy was to be the primary channel for our quest that particular night in May. The quest location, which is somewhere in Quezon City, is nestled amongst the bustling gigantic malls in this quiet and peaceful city.

Mrs. Wong decided to move to her new home owing to its convenient location and its proximity to other major locations in the city.

Spacious and not yet very much populated at that time, her 2-storey, detached apartment unit stood tall and proud in the area. Thanks to its expansive and assertive balcony, its colossal front door that is elaborately carved with laurels and ferns and its princely windows, the frontage of her house seems to overlook the property's entire expanse. Its lightly coloured foyer and wide garden space also gave it a unique personality.

My appreciation of the entire development was eventually halted when I heard Tony say to me, "Look at the balcony using your third eye, do you see anything?" while simultaneously pointing to the centre of my forehead just above my eyebrows.

"There seems to be 2 figures up there" I said.

'"Do you hear anything? Use your psychic ear," Tony countered while pointing to a spot about one inch above my ear, slightly forward.

"I hear noises, a shout for help," I reported.

"There are actually three spirits on the balcony," Tony confirmed "and an elemental also lives in the small palm tree." Our quest agent, Mrs. J. Wong, arrived soon after. Tony then made a round of introductions.

Prior to entering the gates made of twisted metal bars which are kept locked, Mrs. Wong told us that the house is still under construction and they still can't finish it because unnatural circumstances kept occurring in the place.

She reports that painters and carpenters would always get sick, one after the other. The following day, paint smudges would often appear on newly painted walls. As such, the house continued to be incomplete up to this time.

When the house gates and doors were opened, Tony asked Perla, Buddy, Jenny, Zaldy and me to scan the house.

Perla is a strong channel and psychic. Her strong senses have always been required for exceptional cases -- such as this one. Jenny, on the other hand, is a graduate of Tony's Magick class. A young lady who always wears a smile on her face, Jenny never fails to make the saddest of moods glow and smile. Jenny occasionally does Oracle readings and magick spells. Zaldy, a high school student, is the youngest member of our group.

Upon entering the house, I immediately felt suffocated. The air is stale and the house seemed to overflow with the presence of an unknown negative energy. We moved around the ground floor, scanning it all at the same time as we normally do. After sometime, Buddy led the way to the first floor where the bedrooms are located.

On the edge of the stairs in the first floor, a room to my right that was painted in blue got my attention. While the others were preoccupied with the other rooms, I became strongly attracted to this particular room, as if someone or something is pulling me towards it.

The blue room is situated in the far corner of the house. The cabinets are built-in next to the door, and its windows are located on the far side of the wall. Despite the non-functioning fluorescent lamp, the room's blue interior is barely visible because of light coming from the hallway. As I entered the room, I immediately felt my body hairs stand on its roots. I also felt very, very cold.

At the far corner of the room, I caught a glimpse of some hazy figures. I felt threatened at this point, so I decided to slowly back out without saying a word to anyone. I kept this particular sensation to myself, for possible validation afterwards.

As I moved to the other rooms, Buddy also chanced upon the blue room where I had just been. "Wow! Hey guys, take a look in here," he said.

The rest of the group followed Buddy to the blue room, and this is where we've unanimously decided to locate the circle. We informed Tony that we have singled out the blue room because this is the place where the strongest energy is.

As we started bringing chairs to the blue room, the group happened to overlook one other room downstairs that was presumably the master's bedroom. Inside the relatively darkened room is a queen-sized brass bed. En-suite is a bath around the blind far corner.

Tony and the rest of the group scanned this particular room, to where we again decided to have the circle ew-located. When I tried entering the room after the others had already left, I was taken aback. It is as if an invisible force field is blocking my way. I got perplexed mainly because of the strong magnetic-like energy inside the room.

Tony asked, "Is this room less energised than the blue room?"

"No," was our chorused response.

Our group thus decided to locate the circle in this particular room. As we confined ourselves inside the master's bedroom, Tony began to pre-arrange everybody within the circle. Buddy sat directly in front of me. The entire house lights were doused off; five candles were lighted then placed in the centre of the circle. Zaldy has specifically arranged for it to be in a Star of David formation. We then commenced.

"Imagine that the top of your head is the opening of a vase," began Tony. "Yes," I said.

"Now what do you sense," came the next question.

"A fog or a mist of sorts it is trying to move in and out of the mouth of the vase," I replied.

With the use of a brass bell and an Indian rattle, Tony then tried to summon the presence to the circle.

The high-pitched sound of the brass bell is loud and strong enough to permeate into the inner sanctum of oneself. Its sound awakens any individual's psychic hearing and desire to be one with the sound.

On the other hand, the Indian rattle is so rustic in its resonance that it seemed like we are listening to a worn out wooden crackle. Its rattling sound seems to fill the room with nature's energy and presence. The sound of crackling objects inside the hollowed shell, meanwhile, is so alluring and seemed to be attracting attention to itself.

Yet, Tony was unsuccessful in enticing the presence. I also noticed the five candles as they continued burning fervently and fiercely at the centre of the circle.

Upon Tony's suggestion, Zaldy doused the candles off with his fingers. With magick, one is not supposed to blow candles for it is believed that doing so will give any black magician a chance to seize a part of your breath or life for its own purposes.

Darkness soon fell upon us. The only glow that filtered into the room, entering by the window, is light coming from the nearby street.

A sudden chilling sensation then enveloped us. The room's collective atmosphere became one with the group. It feels like the room is now a part of us and that we ourselves are a part of the essence of the room. The elemental is now amongst us. A presence of unknown energy can distinctively be felt moving around the room.

The elemental, in particular, is moving behind us at the circle's outer border. It initially wanted Tony to be the channel but was requested to move on to Buddy.

Soon after Buddy's confirmation that the energy is already within him, I physically opened my eyes. I discerned a tall and dark shadowy figure behind Buddy.

I could not sense whether it is human spirit or elemental. Human spirits are basically a form of energy presence that comes from a previous human incarnation. More often than not, human spirits are those of the deceased who have chosen to remain earth-bound for a number of reasons.

On the other hand, elementals are a kind of energy presence that is not directly connected with human incarnations. Therefore, they are not of human origins. Elementals are classified as a form of energy that are personified or manifested from basic elements known in the East.

Thus an elemental can either be air, water, fire or earth. Deeper mystical knowledge adds ether as another form of element which, generally speaking, is a combination of one or more of the basic elements.

Further subdivisions and/or sub-classifications are also present in each element.

Looking at Buddy's silhouette more diffusely, I can see another shadowy figure. Beyond this shadow, certain other characteristics unfold along with Buddy's own shadow form. Shapes, colours and other pertinent descriptions eventually manifest as I continued to gaze at Buddy.

Soon, I see a large cephalic creature standing in front of me. Its head is so large that it almost touches the ceiling. It supports a sort of cape from its broad shoulders. It has no facial features except for equally large, pointed eyes.

Initially, I wondered what these visions were and where they came from. However, I didn't utter a single word and just kept the visions to myself.

Tony then broke the silence, saying: "Buddy, describe the entity." Buddy described the elemental that was with us that night as follows:

"7 to 8 feet tall; red, fiery eyes; cloaked; wears a one-layer head dress with violet dress and necklace; has a violet-coloured stone on the necklace; carries a long walking stick, with consorts; and is shadowy with extensive head extensions."

A greeting is the spirit questors' means of giving respect. It is our way of emphasizing that we are present not to banish or send them away, but to help work out a better relationship between them and those that they have disturbed.

Through Buddy, the elemental expressed anger and disappointment over the disrespect accorded by the occupants to him.

Meantime, Tony is already trying to decipher the kind of elemental that we have. Based on Buddy's elaborate descriptions of the elemental, Tony surmised it was an air elemental.

The Chinese always believed in four kinds of elements: water, earth, fire and air. Chinese folklore believes living and non-living things are basically made up of all these elements. To a certain extent, apportionment of each element can help determine the characteristics of the said being.

When asked what it wanted, it first and foremost asks for a mini-house on the highest point of the roof. Being an air element, it obviously wants something close to its prime life-source.

It also wants things that are associated with air. The elemental, among others, asked for hanging plants, wind chimes, incense offerings and banners.

DERICKSIDO

"What type of banners?" Tony queried.

With my eyes closed, a shape started to flash quickly inside my mind. Unusual and absurd as it may be, I refrained from judging my visions. A pendant banner kept on flashing in my mind's eye. The colour yellow and orange also kept appearing. It is triangular in shape. I maintained my silence. Soon after, the other channels confirmed to Tony that the banners should be triangular in shape.

Throughout the quest, I could physically feel quick rushes of draught passing behind me. One time, I felt a tug at my right hand as if trying to free up my hand away from that of the person beside me. I could also distinctively feel my head being pulled back even as I struggled to straighten it. Both my shoulders also felt unnaturally heavy.

My left ear also felt ticklish throughout the quest. Apart from the eerie silence and the conversations between Tony and the members of the circle, I distinctively heard distant incomprehensible shouts and deep, short and heavy breathing.

"What is the name of the elemental?" Tony queried again.

Much like the letters of the alphabet prominently displayed in primary school, the letters of the alphabet flashed inside my mind. At random, certain letters seemed to flash and distinguish itself from the other letters. **C-H-E-L-I-O-G**.

I initially thought I just made up that name. But a few seconds later, Buddy answered Tony, "His name is spelled as **C-H-E-L-E-V-I-O**." Close enough, I told myself.

With practically all the details of what we wanted already answered by the elemental, Tony eventually asked us to close the circle. From Tony, counter-clockwise, each one of us inside the circle uttered their respect and thanks.

Immediately after the circle was closed, the feeling of heaviness and dissent that I felt earlier was gone. The atmosphere is now light, and my initial feeling of suffocation is now gone. Before the night ended, Mrs. Wong offered us late night snacks somewhere in Tomas Morato Avenue. Together with a friend, I decided to ride along with her.

On the way, I felt uneasy. I kept sensing another being inside the car. There were literally just three of us, but I sensed a fourth being.

The fourth being is a female. I strongly felt her on the rear passenger seat beside the agent's friend. A follower, a friend, or an entity seeking help? I don't know, as this was only my first quest beyond existence.

Tony must have sensed my perplexity and my constant queries about the supernatural. During the late night snack at the diner, the events of my first quest kept repeating inside my mind.

It was a totally different experience. It gave me a new point of view at looking at things. Before parting ways at that early morning affair, Tony gave me a smooth white stone known locally as "*batong buhay*". I insisted on knowing its purpose, to which Tony replied, "It contains a power of its own. You will know its purpose in the future. Always bring that stone with you...it will help protect you."

At that, I thanked him.

"By the way, two or three more quests and you will start to channel." Not knowing what he meant, I went home still a little puzzled.

The week that followed my first official quest is full of unexpected events. Herein is the content of my personal journal:

21 May (Wednesday)

"I barely had enough sleep last night. In fact, I was not able to sleep at all. Last night, I experienced something which I could not explain.

At around 10 p.m., I am at the mezzanine room studying and reading some materials related to work. I am sitting in bed which directly faced the 10-step wooden stairs.

I grew up in this rather old 1950's apartment. The wooden stairs leading to the mezzanine room exhibited a particular quality common of post-war apartments.

The wooden stairs resonate with a unique sound when someone goes up or down its steps. The whole mezzanine would slightly "vibrate" due to the weight applied on the connecting stairs.

Last night, I am bothered by the mass visit of unseen guests. The noise created by the stairs and the subtle movement of the mezzanine floor made me shiver in fright.

No one in the family admitted to being even close to the stairs. The creaking sound is distinguishable.

In my mind's eye, I could see dozens of figures (humans and otherwise) passing by the side of my bed. They are going in all directions.

Having been both frightened and disturbed, I verbally stated that I am doing something and wish not to be disturbed.

I peacefully and gently asked them to go and leave me alone. I then concentrated on what I was doing before. Seven to thirteen minutes later and everything is back to normal. The air is now lighter and I can finally go to sleep.

Last night is a particularly different night. It is not my habit of leaving the lights open when I go to sleep. However, due to the unwanted "courtesy call" I am given by unseen guests, I slept with the lights on. In spite of that, I am still unable to sleep. I repeatedly awakened during the night particularly because I sensed somebody is watching me. More than that, occasional creaking sound can be heard of the floor which snapped me back to full consciousness."

A Love like No Other

"To love & to hold, in sickness and in health, 'til death do us part."

These are the words of oath so sweetly spoken to express our love. Yet, in this troubled world, such a love rarely exists. It might only take a minute to say that promise, but we have a lifetime to fulfil it. There are rarer times when the promise of love does not end with death but rather, continuous even in the after-life.

John and Maureen have been living together for quite some time. Their relationship outside marriage were accepted and respected by friends and family in a nation of predominantly Catholics.

John is an ex-politician in a distant northern Luzon province. He lost in the previous elections and is making plans to seek re-election in the forthcoming local elections.

Maureen is involved in entrepreneurship. She owns a small grocery located in front of her house where she sells mostly imported goods. Profit from this small business is helping augment the couple's daily needs, and everything seemed perfectly alright for them. Until one day...

An assassin's bullet finally shattered the simple, happy and humble life of this lovely couple. John's assassins' were very accurate. With just a single bullet to his head, he died right on the spot. Witnesses did not bother to intervene for fear of reprisal.

From that tragic day onwards, Maureen's life and dreams were put in chaos. Two months after John's death, Maureen's family decided to seek the intervention of the Spirit Questors.

At that time, I have only been with the Sprit Questors for more than a month. I still had to learn lots of things about being a real questor. Learning, after all, is a continuous process.

While it is the questors' policy to avoid cases that involves murder, Tony has decided to process this because of its disturbing effects on the living. As a Spirit Questor, Tony is primarily concerned over the present state of the spirit.

Somehow, John is disturbing the general way of living of the family he had left behind. Maureen has reported that John's presence is so strong that she felt uneasy and possessed.

The quest was scheduled on June 6, 1997. Our group decided to meet in Cubao at 6 p.m. With us were Tracy and Lory.

Tracy is a senior channel and a graduate of Tony's magick class.

Lory, on the other hand, is a communications graduate teaching literature to high school students. She is also a channel and a psychic.

Normally, it would take just four-hours to travel from Manila all the way to San Jose City in Nueva Ecija. However, for unknown reasons and due to unprecedented traffic, we reached San Jose City at 2 a.m.

The road leading to Maureen's house is about 8-kilometers from the city centre. It took us another 20 minutes to find Maureen's house, passing through totally dark and winding road.

Relaxing and focusing more closely, I saw the surrounding darkness of open fields as an eerie, hair-raising playground for shadows and dark figures.

The scenery also reminded me of convocation of sorts, more like a caucus of various elementals and entities.

Along the way, numerous dwarves and *kapres* abound. My visions of them include dwarves playing mischievously, while the *kapres* would simply be relaxing by the roadside or chasing one another.

For someone like me who has not yet fully developed control over his psychic senses, these visions would often come and go through the corner of one's eye.

The *kapre* would appear as huge shadows or forms, appearing in various densities. Other entities can be seen as formless black mists or hazy yet distinct silhouettes.

Dwarves, on the other hand, would appear as partly luminescent form or shadow figures. In the rich blackness of the area, they are often hard to see.

Other elementals joined us in the trip. From where I was looking, I was surprised to see a figure just outside the window. I am sure it was not my own reflection, or any of those inside the van. Then, as suddenly as it appeared, the figure eventually faded away.

Soon, we arrived at Racquel's home, Maureen's sister. Racquel lived in a small country-town in the outskirts of San Jose City. At first glance, her house looks just as ordinary as that of everyone else's, very typical of a country-house with only the bare essentials.

A small walk-in convenience store prominently fronts the place. At this time of the night, the neighbourhood is immaculately silent, with only the occasional barking of the dogs shattering the stillness of the night.

The light breeze is refreshingly cool. The clear dark sky and a few lighted streetlights give an ethereal illumination. On this particular night of our quest, there was no moon to gaze at.

We spent some time stretching our aching legs from the gruelling 8-hour journey. Not wanting to lose any more time, Tony immediately asked Racquel to show us the place where John got assassinated.

Thinking that it was only about a few minutes away, Tony wanted to see the place right away to be able to make necessary adjustments in the quest.

Surprisingly, approximately just 10 to 15 steps away from Racquel's house, at the corner of the main road and the road leading to John's place, is the exact place where John was gunned down. Instinctively, Tony and the rest of the group began to psychically scan the area to see if any of John's memory or psychic remnants was still there.

Psychically sensing an area or object is very much like scanning it. The psychic senses are focused on the area or object and whatever perceptions or impressions gathered are magnified.

It is similar to looking at the area or object holistically and then re-focusing on its stronger energy or vibrations. John's psychic ashes are present but it is weak and is relatively being overpowered by other forces in the area.

Logically, the only remaining place where John's psychic remains may still be at its strongest is at the local cemetery where he was buried.

Thus, as soon as Tony announced that the quest would be held at the public cemetery where John was buried, everybody's face turned stone-cold. Etched on our faces were stupefaction, fear and surprise.

A quest at the local cemetery is logical, but holding a séance at the cemetery (and in the middle of the night at that!) is completely sur-real. For the record, this was to be the first official spirit quest at a cemetery.

Soon after a short trip to the local motel to drop off our things and for a quick freshen up, the group headed back to Racquel's place, and into that now familiar dark and winding road.

Our destination this time is the local cemetery where John was buried.

Maureen, Trixie, Racquel, Erwin and a driver-friend of the family accompanied us. The trip to the local cemetery is short and bumpy but when we arrived, it was already 45-minutes past 2 a.m.

Although located at the far end of the village, the local cemetery is nestled amidst a large piece of government property being surrounded by numerous overgrown trees. Surrounding the age-old trees were more vast open spaces as far as one can imagine.

The cemetery was in total darkness -- so dark you can not even see your own hands in front of you. Equally ghostly and deafening is the sound of silence.

Tony tried to ease the surmounting tension a little bit by asking the driver, in a jest, to turn off the radio lest we disturb those resting in peace and eventually awaken them.

As the van slowly entered the cemetery gates, which normally were left unlocked, we saw tombstones of all shapes and sizes starting to envelop us completely. Whitewashed and eerily still, the tombstones stood under equally haunting crosses and other ghostly sculptures.

The van stopped right at the very centre of the whole place, near a huge lonesome Acacia tree. In the high-pitched sound of silence and darkness, we queued out of the van one after the other.

We requested the driver to leave the van's lights on as this was to be our only source of light. Without the lights on, we stand at a loss in the middle of necropolis in total darkness. We all walked together along the pebble filled walkway, towards the family mausoleum. It took us between 4-5 minutes to reach the far end of the cemetery where John's remains were buried.

In the ensuing darkness around us with only the van's headlights to illuminate our way, a pale outline of a luminescent character slowly formed a few yards ahead of us. It drifted gently towards us until all of us could see it floating on top. As it came nearer, it began to take shape and color -- it was a fairy! It greeted Tony and the rest of the members of our group.

The sight of a fairy gives off a feeling of happiness and excitement.

The fairy is accompanied by dozens of small pixies simultaneously floating and moving around.

They are similar to orbs normally seen in pictures and videos. The fairy wore a distinctively bright sort of material as cover. A long matted, hair-like object extends from its head and into the body. I sensed a feeling of welcome and invitation at the same time.

When I looked around, I saw that everybody is still grouped closely together. Despite the complete standstill of the wind as evidenced by the leaves of the trees, cold light wind still blew past us.

Though there were only 9 of us present at the cemetery that time, the noise created by walking on the pebble-strewn walkway resembled that of a group of around 20 to 25 people. Surely, these sounds should be coming from somewhere else.

Then it came. Tony blurted out that somebody was holding on to his right shoulder.

Tracy reports of a sensation of a similar cold grip on her left arm followed by a hard tag. Furthermore, she says she felt a sharp strong and steady push from behind.

Tracy describes it as though she was impatiently being pushed forward, like someone being asked to move faster. For her part, Lory remembers feeling a playful entity running a cold sensation up and down her right arm.

Further on, we hear subtle echoic moans and groans from around us. There were other spirits who have nonchalantly decided to meet us at the gravelled path and collide with our group head-on. Their faces were right in front of our faces.

While Tracy is struggling to keep her psychic senses closed, my own psychic perception heightened. From the corner of my eyes, I saw about 3 to 5 indistinct forms.

A few of them were slowly rising from the earth while the others simply stood beside their tombstones and grave markers. The creatures varied in appearance.

I decided to refocus my vision on the three forms I saw. Slowly and eventually with much better clarity, I saw 3 male-like figures. One was dressed in a formal coat and tie. Nonetheless, the lower half of his body was not completely visible. His lower limbs, from the thigh down to his feet, blended with the darkness. I sensed delight and a

gentle smile.

The other mist form I saw was that of a younger looking male who was probably in his late 20s or early 30s.

He was wearing a tattered shirt with stains around it. I assumed that he was stabbed to death as I felt a momentary sharp sensation on my torso.

Bruises and blood also covered his face, which equally showed anguish and an emotive call for help. I gathered that this spirit is actually asking for help. He offensively went near our group but did not do any harm, except to scare the wits out of me.

The last of the three spirits I saw was that of a man with a dark intent. Located slightly to my right, he slowly stood up from behind a tombstone.

In fact, he floated slowly until he was standing up. His manner of rising can be described as that of being perfectly straight and perpendicular to the tomb.

When he faced our group, I saw that half his face was decomposing as fast as that of the other half of his body. He then managed to smile as he slowly floated towards us onto the gravelled walkway in front of us. He stood directly in front as we walked forward.

The group was not entirely aware of his presence. We passed right through him and soon after that, he disappeared.

Tony stopped and viewed the distant area where we were to hold a quest. He noted that there were too many conflicting energies that could overpower our purpose.

I added that I sensed a strong and dissenting essence residing on the huge tree immediately behind John's mausoleum.

It does not wish to be disturbed at the moment. Just then, from out of the blue, John's thoughts crossed mine. He said that he would like the quest to be done at home for the safety of his relatives.

I told Tony about my sudden thoughts. Tony agreed and we traced our steps back to the van.

While we moved in and out of the maze of tombstones, I continued to see ethereal forms with my psychic and physical eyes.

Other unearthly forms continued to weave in and out of the tomb-stones, mausoleums and markers. They moved in various tempos. While others were visible only from the waist, the others were completely hazy and some, even formless.

I kept silent on these phantasmal visions as it might further scare our agents.

On our way back to the house, the driver noted that the van was unusually heavy as the engine revved much more than before.

The van slowly edged towards the main cemetery gate when, for no apparent reason at all, the accelerator pedal got stuck.

Good thing the driver was alert and was able to find a way to save us all from eventually talking to John and the others, face to face.

It was now 3:40 in the morning. We all held hands and formed a circle at Racquel's living room. Tracy lighted two white candles and placed it in the centre of the circle.

Beside the candles is a coloured 8 by 11 inches portrait of John.

"Is he here?" Tony asked. I replied in the positive.

John was observing from behind me and walked counter-clockwise. In my mind's eye, I saw him wearing a grayish-black overcoat.

He was observant about what we were doing. Tracy further described John as wearing a shining white dress. He has his arms crossed on his chest.

John wanted to tell Maureen something very important. I felt a sense of urgency.

Tracy channelled while Lory and I acted as secondary channels.

We took turns greeting John. He explained that he was not in any pain and that he is already on his way to the light.

He joined us because he wanted to tell Maureen something that would eventually help her.

At this point, Tony emphasized that John has only about 15 minutes left before he is required to withdraw back into the light.

How Tony knew about this is something I do not know.

"Maureen, I will always love you even if I'm not with you right now," John said through Tracy.

John wanted Maureen to know that he will always be guarding and helping her in this lifetime. She need not worry as he is perfectly all right.

Furthermore, John specifically requests Maureen to unconditionally forgive the people responsible for his death. It would only hold him down if she will not forgive them. Maureen is crying profusely now.

She recalls having strongly felt John's presence as well as love for her. Tony then intervened and explicitly explained to Maureen the need for love and forgiveness.

He told Maureen the consequences if she will not heed John's advice.

In between sobs, Maureen slowly acknowledged having understood John's message. Though hard at first, she was able to let go of John and eventually set him free. Shortly thereafter, John had to go.

I saw him slowly withdrawing back into a distant light away from us.

"Maureen, I love you so much and will love you forever," cried John.

"I love you, too," Maureen answers, now weeping uncontrollably.

"Thank you very much. I love you," were John's parting words, an understanding and passionate declaration of his love for Maureen, which he expressed through me.

I then lost contact with him, but I could clearly see him slowly being engulfed by a significantly bright light.

He moved farther away from us until he eventually disappeared. He was now happy and at peace.

We broke the circle and were quiet for sometime. We felt nostalgic about the whole experience.

I then asked Racquel what John wore when he was buried.

Racquel described his burial dress as a grayish-black overcoat with a green-stripped undershirt.

This explains my visions of John at the start of the quest when I first saw him.

The quest that transpired here is clearly an example of a love that is unquestionably beyond the promise of "...'til death do us part."

It is a love that has touched them once yet lasted more than a lifetime. It is a kind of love unheard of in this crazy world of materialism.

John showed us the true meaning of unconditional forgiveness, and of undying love.

A love devoid of time and space. A promise said in so short a time yet fulfilled even after a lifetime.

It is a promise left unsaid when he was still alive.

An unfinished business. It is a love unofficially recognised by the world of man and human law. A love taboo for the social milieu of marriages and ceremonies.

A love more lasting and enduring, even further in the afterlife.

Ilocos

Much like a candle lighted in total darkness during a quest, the spirit questor's noble endeavor often shines brightly in the end.

People from all places want our group to hold a quest in their midst.

To help them let go of a dearly departed, to find peace in their household, to simply learn about this world and beyond – these are only some of the reasons why people have come to us for assistance in the past.

The lure of eager students and a chance to be close with them set the string of events for a seminar-quest in the northern province of Ilocos Norte, the land of native shamans and naturally open psychics.

Virtually left behind due to a string of unexpected events that usually happens to out of town quests, I was able to catch up with a group of eight questors somewhere along Mindanao Ave. in Quezon City.

Soon after a short stop-over, we eventually resumed the journey.

A recent tropical storm destroyed a major bridge connecting Ilocos Sur to Ilocos Norte. The damage caused on the major thoroughfare forced us to wait alongside the motorway for a few hours. To pass time away, some of the questors practiced various psychic exercises.

The isolation of the place in addition to the total darkness gave us the necessary psychic stimulus to exercise our psychic senses. During the individual activity, we managed to sense that the area is full of unseen natural spirits. Though eerily silent and still, the night permeated an atmosphere of fellowship and companionship. Looking further through the inner senses, the festive flock of unseen beings give a sense of suffocation and heaviness amidst the open and wide landscape around us. Being the end of a working week, some of the questors also opted to sleep inside the van and generally re-charge their physical energies.

A blinding light forced its way to my half-closed eyes. I tried to open my eyes but the sun's immense brightness made me close it again. The cold, fresh mountain air pierced my otherwise smog-filled nostrils and brushed heavily against my face.

We are now barely just an hour or two away from our final destination.

Again, as I opened my eyes to the light, the early morning breeze and sunlight gave me a fresh new feeling.

Accustomed to urban life, the contrasting scenery of rolling mountains and flat terrains made me wonder out loud about the simplicity of life in the countryside. In a way, it has brought me closer to a world that is completely different from that which I used to know.

In a sense, it has brought me to two different worlds. Spirit questing, in essence, is very much the same -- a simple way of communicating with another world.

Between the world of mortals and the spirit, the lines of interaction are always open, and all it takes is unpretentious thinking and for us to keep an open mind.

Arriving at 7 in the morning from a back-breaking 16-hour road trip, I barely had time for a quick nap. The seminar begins at 8:30 a.m.

Deus Vox College sits at the heart of Laoag City. Its grilled fences gave us a heart-warming view of the wide-open spaces the college has to offer.

Within the leaves-strewn yard of the campus were a number of wood-en benches shaded by huge trees. It provided students a way of keep-ing in touch with nature, and with oneself.

Our hosts, Dr. Jaycee, president for academic affairs of the Deus Vox College and Fr. John, SVD, received us warmly at the Savior House.

A sumptuous breakfast of native sausages and fried rice pre-empted our activities for the day. On the college's front gate is a banner in-forming the public of the day's seminar-workshop.

WELCOME PARTICIPANTS AND GUESTS TO A SEMINAR-WORKSHOP ON DEVELOPING YOUR PSYHIC POWERS CONDUCTED BY TONY PEREZ AND THE SPIRIT QUESTORS

Close to about 118 participants registered for the activity.

Fr. John, Dr. Jaycee and other faculty members and staff members of the college also attended the workshop.

The number of attendees who showed interest in the paranormal and the occult overwhelmed us. Tony did not expect it to be this much. The enthusiasm of participants flowed unceasingly throughout the seminar.

Eventually, the organizers of the event had to turn down other interested participants.

Tony began the seminar with a few introductory words describing the paranormal and the occult, differentiating the views and various ideas concerning each concept.

He also elaborated on misconceptions about psychic phenomenon.

To start with, there are four psychic senses as there are five-physical senses. Science has taught us that we have various senses for seeing, smelling, tasting, feeling and hearing.

Similarly, each one is gifted with his own set of senses for use with the inner self. These senses are collectively known as psychic senses, and are often generally "mis-termed" as the third eye or inner eye.

For some reason, however, the use of our psychic senses has become restricted and repressed in this worldly existence.

Clairaudience is a term used for hearing with the inner ear. The "psychic ear" is situated approximately one-inch above and slightly forwards the physical ear.

Hearing with the psychic ear is relatively hard and must clearly be differentiated from normal sounds we hear.

Another form of utilizing the psychic sense is that of seeing objects, things or spirits. The appellation for such gift is Clairvoyance.

The third eye is traditionally situated in the centre of the forehead, about an inch above the brow line.

Seeing with the inner eye or third eye is more laborious and takes more time to develop and to perfect.

Occasionally, a quick flash or vision from the corner of ones physical eyes is significant for a temporary blinking of the third eye.

The other psychic senses known are the psychic feeling and psychic intuition. Psychic feeling can easily be identified in ourselves when a general feeling of physiologic reaction takes place in our physical body, like when our body hairs stand on its ends – we commonly call this as "goose bumps."

Although certain logical reasons should first be eliminated, the end-point is generally a psychic feeling of some unknown presence.

It is also imperative to say that not all psychic feeling reactions can be attributed to spirits or to other unknown presence. Psychic feeling also involves the ability to acquire emotions presented by the spirit or the elemental.

Finally, psychic intuition is different from psychic feeling in the way logic affects both.

In psychic feeling, logic tells us that we feel sad, happy or angry for some unknown reasons.

Psychic intuition, on the other hand, is not in any way logical. Psychic intuition is more of being instinctive and reactive.

The seminar-workshop on developing the psychic senses centres on the awakening in each participant of these senses.

Throughout the seminar, Tony guides and offers assistance in the opening of these senses. He uses a variety of methods: a rattle, a gong, a candle, a scrying disc, a mirror or a crystal ball are just few of what he utilizes.

It is finally up to the individual to further develop his psychic senses.

Creating the tower of light

To begin the seminar-workshop, the questors guided the group to a tower of light exercise.

It is a process of meditation wherein we gently aid each participant in creating a psychic shield in order for him to be protected from external psychic stimuli and influence.

It is also a form of meditation to help participants relax and prepare themselves and their psychic senses for full utilization.

After the tower of light and relaxation techniques, Tony began the workshop. "Look at me. Look through me."

Using an unfocused stare at Tony, a faint glow of luminous light can be perceived around him, much like a faint halo.

"Does anyone see anything?" Tony asked.

Quite a few of the participants raised their hands to acknowledge that they see a ring of light around him. Generally, this is known as the aura of the individual.

I was leisurely enjoying the vision of various colors emanating from Tony's aura from the side of the platform towards the front when I subtly "saw", from the outer corner of my left eye, a movement from the rear door.

A young man in his early twenties walked hurriedly towards the front from the back. I expected him to come into full view as he neared the stage. As he centered on my direct vision, the hair on my arms stood. He then disappeared just as quickly I saw him.

"Hmmm," I said to myself, "something is going on in here." Suddenly, all my body hairs began to stand on its ends.

"I think somebody is here," I again told myself. Perplexed, I tried to set the thought aside and focus on the activity at hand.

I looked at the other questors who were also performing the exercise.

I caught Macky's attention and telepathically, I knew that he also saw the young man and likewise wondered about him.

Jobert also gave me a quick look signalling that his body hairs were all standing, and that there is a presence within the room.

I smiled and acknowledged their thoughts with a slight court bow.

After the exercise, Tony asked us to take note of participants who are able to clearly see his aura. Following the clairvoyance exercise, Tony went on to discuss about the clairaudience part.

With the use of a Tibetan singing brass bowl, Tony explained the concept of the bowl and the proper way of using the hum created by it to enable oneself to access the psychic ear.

Slowly, Tony started to uniformly slide the mallet on the brass bowl's outer lip. After just a few strokes, a soft hum started to permeate the tranquillity of the whole media centre.

The hum echoed throughout the walls, becoming louder and louder as Tony continued the motion.

The bowl continued perpetuating a soft hum that soon filled the entire place. Under the soft hum of the Tibetan brass bowl, a very faint but slightly audible sound different from the hum could be heard.

"Help! Help me! Aaaaaahhh..."

The spine-tingling voice of a young male echoed under the constant high-pitched sound of the Tibetan brass bowl. The voice is so deep and hair-raising that it gave all of us goose-bumps. Occasionally, the voice would disappear amidst the hum of the brass bowl.

Then, as suddenly as it disappeared, it will again echo so gravely and deeply as before.

At the end of the exercise, Tony asked the group what our experiences were.

The responses varied and it was not surprising to know that a handful of participants heard the young man's voice.

We again took note of those who were able to hear the voice. For confirmation, Tony asked the questors to elaborate on the voice heard on this exercise and the vision seen on the exercise before.

We then explained that a presence indeed is with us. In fact, it kept on moving around the media centre.

He is a young man in his early 20s, of moderate height, fair complexioned and always on the go. He is lost and wants help in finding his way towards some place.

Surprise and disbelief caught a number of the participants.

A number of them admitted that the media centre is indeed one of the places where they occasionally encounter strange occurrences.

Chairs will be heard moving about inside when nobody is in, lights will turn on and off without anyone touching the switch and a mumbled voice could sometimes be heard inside the room.

All throughout the morning session, when everyone else was busy practicing his or her psychic sights and hearing, Macky kept receiving an image of the ancient one.

Macky can vaguely describe the ancient one, except that the images he received are those of a huge snake of sort. He likewise received images of ancient symbols and meanings. The other questors had similar visions of lesser magnitude and degree.

On the other hand, I obtained not a vision of the ancient one or its lesser symbols but of another thing.

The vision is as follows:

> Somewhere within the province, a bus full of youngsters, probably high school students were taking a trip along a small country road. An open field, a rough road and a small wooden bridge comprise the immediate surrounding of the bus' location.

> A lone tree along the road served as the only landmark. The bus, being on a rough road, is travelling leisurely at moderate speed. Upon reaching the wooden bridge, the bus veered excessively to the side of the road causing it to fall on its side and tumble over. I could not see further whether there were any injuries.

The vision came to me in a slow motion manner. It played and replayed the whole scenario twice before coming to an end.

The vision's implication bothered me. I'm not sure whether the vision is an imprint of the past, or is pre-cognitive of a future occurrence. I had no way of knowing.

The rest of the day went smoothly with occasional flashes of the young male participant moving about from one place to another.

I could see him constantly moving from the rear side of the media centre towards the front stage.

Further on during the day, the Spirit Questors helped participants develop their senses on psychic feeling and intuition using various exercises.

After discussing the various psychic senses and eventually guiding the participants on how to access them, an open forum was held. Halfway through the open forum, I suddenly felt extremely cold.

The hairs at the back of my neck started to stand. My ears began to feel icy-cold, and my head felt cold as well. Seated to my left is Bing.

A few seconds later, he gave me a perplexed look and signalled something.

Bing said that his right arm is feeling extremely cold.

His body hairs were all visibly standing up. He adds that he suddenly felt very cold more particularly on this arm compared to his left.

Then, he saw my own sensitivities.

"Is there a spirit in between us?" he inquired. "Yes," I smiled.

"Okay, that's enough. Tell him to go away," he nervously asked me.

"Why? He's done nothing wrong," I said.

"I don't think I can take it any further. I feel cold," he retorted. "For a while, I think he is on to something."

A few minutes later, as suddenly as the rush of cold breeze came, the feeling of coldness subsided.

"He disintegrated just like that," I informed Bing after he gave me a "is he gone?" look.

At the end of the open forum, a young female participant who could no longer contain herself stepped forward and asked for confirmation.

She claims to seeing things that others could not. She admits having heard of the young man's voice during the clairaudience exercise and having seen him as well during the clairvoyance activity.

Lastly, she saw the young man walk slowly towards the stage during the open forum. She reports that from the media center's back area, the young man went up the stage on the right and settled himself between Bing and myself. From there, he stood for a while then in a frolic bent himself forward closer to us. Then, slowly, he vanished.

That girl was Dawn, a junior marketing student. She wants us to verify her visions. Surprised at her accuracy and specifications, I confirmed her visions while reassuring her that these visions were not a product of her imagination. They were in fact, a reality. It turns out that Dawn's psychic senses were naturally open.

Taking advantage of our presence in the province, Dr. Jaycee took the liberty to schedule a number of quests for the night.

After conferring with Tony, she also requested for an actual quest to culminate the seminar–workshop. More than 120 participants were chosen to join us in the activity.

Tony needed to carefully and equally divide the whole group into sub-groups. He wanted each sub-group to be psychically balanced and well controlled by the questors who would be put in-charge of the group.

After deciding on the grouping and location, Tony assigned me and Billy to hold a quest in the house of a certain Emma M. A group of about 20 students were assigned to us.

Unfinished business

Emma M.'s residence is well kept and maintained. Its arched driveway ends with a huge heavy-set wooden door.

Immediately upon entering the main door, I noticed that the interiors of the house were circular in design, with a large glass window in front and with multi-level flooring.

A 15-step stairs on my right lead to the upper rooms, and alongside these stairs was another set of stairs that led to the lower chambers of the house.

From the receiving room, the facade of the upper rooms would entirely become visible owing to its open-hallway design.

Further towards my right, a sliding door can be seen leading to a side-veranda overlooking the spacious backyard.

The descending set of stairs, meanwhile, leads to the lower floors of the house.

It is surprising to know that most of the rooms are interconnected with adjacent doors and passageways.

Low ceiling-ed and windowless, most of the lower rooms were being used by the family. Consequently, the large house dwarfed the small-sized family.

After scanning the whole house, Billy and I decided to locate our circle in one of the upper rooms.

Surprised at our decision, Mrs. M admitted that she and other family members regularly hear noises of unknown origin from these upper rooms; hence, their decision to use the lower rooms.

To facilitate and generate more coverage of the place, Billy suggested that we further sub-divide our group. Ernie would act as his facilitator while Jobert will join me and my group.

We also divided the 20-some students into two groups, taking into account the group's oneness and harmony.

Before we proceeded inside the house, we led our individual group into the transformation of fear and tower of light exercises.

I chose to quest in one of the rooms near the stairs. The room looked unused and seemed uncared for.

The lights did not work, the windows hanged loose, and dust settled everywhere. A small table stood by the broken-down window.

On top of the table, various religious figures lay immaculately still. A few of the statuettes were either chipped or broken into pieces. Technically, the room is still in good condition.

A one-and-a-half meter by one-meter large rectangular mirror arrayed the room's inner wall by the en-suite bathroom. It faced a built-in closet, thereby forming an illusion of a darkened hall inside the room.

After rearranging the bed and the bedside tables to accommodate our group of ten-participants, I began positioning everyone within the circle.

Basically, I tried to balance the energies, alternately seating the weak and the strong. I positioned myself to face the inner chamber of the room where it is darkest and where the huge mirror hanged.

Even before we started, in the far walls of the chamber, I could figure out the shadow of a moderately tall man.

I also scanned a huge mirror from which, to my surprise, a few other shadows slowly materialized beside my own reflection.

The mirror then slowly metamorphosed into a deep whirling tunnel. It then faded out of sight as the tunnel became clearer. The tunnel walls were shiny and bright. It gave me the illusion of depth and brightness.

Not wanting to astral travel deeply into this newly discovered portal, I slowly willed myself back. The next thing I became aware of is that I am standing in front of the darkened mirror.

Further on, as I got more focused and relaxed, I saw another shadowy figure suddenly appear beside the man, a figure that eventually turned out to be a woman.

Instinctively, I felt that a bond existed between both apparitions. The thought of a wedding ceremony soon followed.

I initially did a round of introductions and orally stated my offer of friendship and peace.

Our group also lighted a single candle and placed it at the centre of the circle. I told them that the group does not intend to banish them from the place. I invited them to the circle to talk to us.

At first sceptical of the offer, the male mentally told me that they prefer to stay afar.

Aside from the answer I got, I perceived that the female was trying to restrain someone other than her husband.

I again re-focused and relaxed further.

Further away in the shadowy corners of the inner chamber, a smaller shadow slowly emerged.

"A boy," I mused to myself.

I wanted to call the boy and converse with him instead.

However, deep within me, something told me not to unless I wanted to deal with the male. The patriarch stood still and was observant of our every move.

In my mind's eye, I sent thoughts of query as to, "Why are you still here?"

The answer breezed through me just gently as a soft evening breeze would. "We still have things to do." Unfinished business. Earth bound.

"Do you see any light?"

"Yes. We know about the light, but we're not going in yet," the father figure answered.

Not wanting to force them into the light but rather, on their own free will, I dropped the topic and focused on the place.

Meanwhile, the participants within the group could not catch-up with the proceedings. A few could barely discern the spirits in the shadows. Others could just feel their body hairs stand up while still others felt icy-cold and partially numb.

Throughout the quest, I could feel a surge of fear moving around the circle.

Most of the fear originated from the girl beside Jobert, who, it turns out, became the most frightened in the group.

Clearing my inner thoughts, I asked the figures further, "Why are you staying at this place?"

In a second or two, the answer came. Not in a single answer though or a vision but somehow as a comprehensive and encompassing concept.

They showed me all points of views at the same time.

The visions I saw flashed so fast I was almost not able to discern what they meant -- until much later.

The father figure showed me the whole house, particularly the upper bedrooms. Each greatly amplified vision showed every particular details of the place.

I was seeing the living room yet I am also seeing the upper bedrooms. Everything is in black & white much like an old-fashioned documentary film.

I soon heard a voice, a narrator of some sort. The voice sounded casual and had no emotion. It was very flat, deep and it seemed like it was coming from all over the place.

"Home."

A flash back to the interior of the whole house.

"Home," the voice re-echoed.

Again, I saw the whole house including its maze like ante-rooms, the numerous doors, spacious receiving room and the high-arched ceiling.

Sadness. My emotion suddenly turned from glad to sad. I suddenly felt sad and unhappy at the stillness of the place.

The eerie silence of the place and its placidity again flashed in my mind's eye. Sadness...

Sadness continued to emanate from the walls, the ceiling, the floor, and just about everywhere else.

Then out of nowhere, the voice again reverberated into my inner thoughts.

"But..."

From being black and white, the visions slowly took colors.

While still looking at the entire place from different points of view at the same time, colors started to appear.

Subtly at first, then slowly, each color became bright and lively. Every piece of object is now brightly colored.

The mirror radiated in a blinding light. The statuettes no longer stood still and covered with dust. Each figure radiated a certain energy and passion. No longer was it chipped nor broken into pieces.

To my mind, each figure suddenly became alive in itself. The room is now showered with sunlight and fresh air. A general feeling of peace emanated from the walls and ceilings.

Even at night, the whole house seemed lively and full of love, laughter, harmony and well-being.

The colors continued to brighten, to glow and to radiate. Each hue greatly magnified itself, yet it did not overshadow the other colors. I can now see radiant colors everywhere.

Even the air seems to have color now.

The vision is just so, "...lovely."

Then suddenly, everything turned to black. A total blackout.

Darkness covered the whole place and only the candle lighted the circle.

Visions of home, sadness, and loveliness quickly passed in my inner eye.

Again, I opened my eyes to the darkened inner chamber of the room. Lurking and unmoving within the darkness were still darker shadows.

Now I understand.

Apparently, the family of the shadows we met did not experience a happy family life when they were still alive.

This is their unfinished business. They wanted to make-up for lost time. For them, the M's house is very much like their own. It is their home.

The stillness and loneliness of the place deeply saddened the family. They longed for it to become a place of love, happiness and joy. They envisioned the home to be an abode of exemplary love and happiness.

Then, from my left hand, a sudden surge of fear came about. It is like a sudden surge of electricity meant to shock and awaken the senses.

It came from someone on my left. The feeling is distinct. I scanned the circle.

The initial fear I felt now moved around the circle.

Getting stronger and stronger as it generated energy for itself from the fears and hidden emotions of the group participants, the effect of the initial fear became evident in the physical reactions of those in the circle.

Quite a few were sobbing and tensing their muscles.

I then decided to close the circle since there is nothing more we can do with the spirits. It is now up to their free will to move on. They have lengthily told us what they wanted with the place to keep them appeased.

We ended the quest after giving a short message of thanks to the spirits who communed with us. We then offered a round of prayers for the family and for the spirits who have gathered around us.

By then, Billy's group had been waiting for us for the past 15 minutes. They have conversed with an elemental that eventually became rude and extremely aggressive.

For the safety of the participants, Billy had to prematurely terminate the circle.

We then decided to follow the main group of questors at the Mansion by the Dam. It took us 30-minutes to reach the place.

Macky informed us that the ancient symbols we perceived earlier this morning were related to his quests.

He conversed with Quetzalcoatl, an ancient demigod of the astral plane. After the last group finished its quest, everybody proceeded back to the college for a congregate quest within the grounds.

We all convoyed back to the college where we immediately assembled for dispatching.

"Take your group to the fourth floor and locate your circle there," we were told.

It is now past 11 p.m. and is nearing midnight.

Joining me in my circle were Dawn, Jaycee and Christine, another seminar participant whose psychic senses are also open.

We stealthily moved through the darkened corridors of the building. The building's main light system remained off. We moved around trying to spot a location for the circle.

However, I noticed that every time I find a spot for locating the circle, energies would dwindle and move further to another spot.

I decided to instinctively follow the energy to a point where it eventually settled.

In one of the floor's classroom, the dragnet eventually slowed down to a stop. Finally, I thought I would settle my circle in the same place.

As I moved closer to the center of the room, a darkened shadow silhouette caught the corner of my eye.

It appeared from near the classroom's front and stiffly walked towards the blackboard through the wall of the adjoining classroom.

As a response, I quickly moved out and went to the next room. I cautiously entered the second room.

Luckily, I caught a glimpse of the figure disappear again towards the blackboard wall to the next room. I naturally followed the figure again.

Room 403

The complete darkness of the whole building offered us the much needed assistance in the group's search for a place.

From room 403's door, I could discern a very faint glow. Situated at the far rear corner of the room, I could now see a figure standing steadily and looking at us.

I inched closer to the room's center.

The rest of the group followed and in the process stumbled through tables and chairs. I can see things more clearly now.

The shadow belonged to that of a young male. He sported a clean-cut hair and is neatly shaven. He beckoned me to the center of the classroom.

"We will locate the circle here," I told the group.

I positioned Dawn in front of me. I made her sit herself directly under the center beam of the classroom, nearest the rear.

I located Christine to my left and Jaycee to my right. I then asked the rest of the group to locate in between us.

The shadow remained in the far corner, observing us. We did a round of introduction and greeting.

When we asked for a response, I saw him smile and in a blink moved himself to stand at Dawn's back.

Dawn will channel tonight, I told myself.

"What is your name?" I queried.

Immediately after orally stating the question, I descended to alpha level and attuned to the spirit and his response.

"Ricardo" is the thought I perceived.

I then descended to the conscious level and just in time, "Ric-ar-do?"

Dawn answered uncertainly.

Her level of accuracy and attunement surprised me even more.

I paused for a while to look at Dawn. I looked at her aura, and she radiated a faint and subtle ethereal glow.

"Are you the presence manifesting in this place?" I asked again.

Earlier that day some students informed us that they occasionally saw a figure come and go from this side of the building.

That someone will abruptly appear and disappear, eventually scaring away the students.

"I am," answered Dawn even before I could ascend to alpha.

Since the quest is a culminating activity of the seminar-workshop, I then asked anyone from the group if they can "see" or "hear" the spirit amongst us. Quite a few acknowledged in the affirmative.

Others even stressed further of the peculiarities of the atmosphere. They expressed extreme coldness of the immediate surroundings.

Heightening my physical and psychic senses, I indeed felt a change in room temperature and even felt a slight breeze brush my face.

In the process, I envisioned an elemental outside the room's outer window.

The elemental is simply watching us and is partially responsible for the slight breeze. Out of fun, the elemental blew air just to try and scare some of the participants.

At the same instant, I discerned a sudden glow of faint light on my right, about 6-feet in front and 7-feet above us.

In relation to Dawn, the faint light emanated from above her left shoulder.

I wanted to know why or what is holding Ricardo earthbound so I asked, "Dawn, what is his dominant emotion? How does he feel?"

"He is not in any pain, just lonely," replied Dulce.

I waited for her to continue and gather more information. "I see a girl and a group of friends."

"A girlfriend?" I asked. "Sort of," Dawn remarked.

"Does he miss them?" "Yes," Dawn answered strongly.

"Ricardo, do you see any light around you?" I gently asked. Silence.

"Do you mean a light similar to this one?" Dawn replied.

I attuned myself to Ricardo and his expressionless face seemed more serene now than before. He pointed to the faint glow of white light to his left and slightly above him.

Clearly now, his features became more profound. He is of medium height, fair complexioned, chinky-eyed and had a sporty-looking hair-cut.

He is pointing to the ethereal light behind Dawn.

"Yes," I said.

A gentle, "of course, isn't it obvious," smile registered on his face.

I casually smiled at him, then asked, "Would you like to move on?"

"I will," was the response.

I then asked the participants in the circle to mentally picture a beam of love from their hearts, going out towards Ricardo.

This, I said, will help hasten his move towards the light. A few minutes passed by, in total silence.

"He is moving, I can see him," Dawn said excitedly.
"There he is," she enthusiastically narrated to the group.

In my mind's eye, I saw Ricardo move towards the source of light.

A smile is clearly etched in his face. A feeling of happiness and joy confounded me as I saw him move.

Dawn must have picked-up on his emotions as she herself physically manifested extreme happiness. Her voice was jittery and fluctuated in excitement and enthusiasm.

In the darkened limbo of my inner mind, Ricardo slowly faded into the light as he moved further on.

He stopped briefly, turned around, and then waved us goodbye.

"Thank you," I said at last before he finally disappeared.

Deep inside, I smiled and said a prayer for him. I've expected the light to eventually fade away but I became concerned when it did not.

A few seconds later from deep within the recesses of the light, another figure suddenly appeared.

Small at first, then gradually growing bigger as it came closer to us.

"Anything more?" I asked Dawn.

By now, I can clearly see that the being from the light is a girl of about 14-16 years old. She is very beautiful.

Her smile is captivating and her eyes twinkled differently. She radiated a dominant feeling of happiness and satisfaction.

Her moves are smooth and fluid-like and her shoulder length hair was brushed lightly against her face.

She gingerly approached the circle and lingered near Dawn.

"There is another presence. I can feel it," Dawn answered.

"What is it?" I asked.

"I do not know," she replied, then continued after a pause, "I feel very cold now and my shoulders feel heavy."

I informed the group that we have a new presence within the circle.

"Right now, she is holding and leaning onto your shoulder," I informed Dawn.

I then asked her to "Attune yourself to her. Tell me her name."

Dawn was silent for a few seconds. Then she voiced out, "Clar... issa..."

"Clarissa has already moved on just recently. She just wants to play around for a while," I said.

Dawn must have already focused and attuned herself to Clarissa as she informed the group further that, "She is kind and gentle. She means no harm."

At that instance, Clarissa playfully moved from Dawn to a male participant at her left. She leisurely fidgeted with him and with another male participant.

She blew air into their face and into their napes. The male participant did verbalize that he felt very cold and could distinctly feel a slight pressure on his shoulder.

Clarissa went about to 'play' with the other participants when a female participant turned hysterical as she neared her.

"She is here. She is touching and holding the back of my head. I could feel it," the girl sobbed hysterically.

I immediately attuned to Clarissa and told her that we need to go and close the circle. She was reluctant and sad. She was just having fun.

I thanked her for the time she spent with us that night, telling her that this would be a night to remember.

I reminded her that she does not belong in this plane of existence anymore but in another. I further told her that she could choose to act as a guide and protector of students in campus.

She also thanked us for giving her time. Finally, I closed the circle of light and broke the circle.

Before finally calling it a night, I suggested that a round of prayers be offered for the souls of Ricardo, Clarissa and the other spirits.

Dawn led the group in that prayer. I clearly felt that each one prayed so intensely that it gave them a new meaning for the act of praying.

They have just been in an experience never usually encountered by anyone so their reverence and respect for the unseen is now changed completely.

We finished the quest at 12:30 a.m. In the early hours of that Sunday, June 29, we were given another point of view in life.

Supplemental to the quest experience is the profound and explicit enlightenment that Fr. John gave us in the early morning mass.

As we celebrated the feast day of St. Paul the Apostle, Fr. John has perfectly "paragon-ed" the questors as the modern day St. Pauls.

While we differ on our approach to the Almighty, we embody the ideals of St. Paul, who himself was a non-traditionalist in his time. The liturgy gave me a new meaning and perspective in dealing with life, and with the gifts that questors have.

Up to this day, the word of encouragement and inspiration still echoed within me.

Our sojourn to Ilocos Norte to help enlighten people about the spirit world has made a complete turnaround.

We were instead the ones who became enlightened, guided further by the very person whom we expected most to disagree with us and with what we do.

A few days later, Tony told me that Jaycee did a background check on the entities that we've communed with on that particular night.

Jaycee enthusiastically informed us that a student named Ricardo has indeed just died. He fitted perfectly our description of him.

She also found out that room 403 is the subject-room where he last enrolled in before he died.

Further on, Jayce also confirmed that there was a student named Clarissa who, prior to her demise, was enrolled in that college.

Before leaving and finally culminating the day's activity, I gave my special bell necklace to a participant named Criselda for her protection and guidance.

With it, she could be spared from any harm and it will eventually hasten the opening of her inner senses.

The bell will also be very useful and could even become a powerful tool if charged and used properly. It could either dispel or attract spirits and elements.

As for Dawn, I decided to give her a previously charged granite stone to help strengthen her psychic senses and her grounding.

It will always keep her in touch with reality, and she would still able to manage her psychic senses.

I likewise passed on to Christine the white polished stone previously given to me by Tony on the night of my first quest.

As it helped me further open my psychic senses and helped dispel any fear that may reside in me, it would do the same to her provided she uses it properly.

The stone would also act as magnetizer for whatever fear she will harness.

In return, Jobert unexpectedly gave me a metallic figure of a Pixie Fairy. It is made of pewter and was exquisitely moulded and crafted to the finest details.

The trip back to Manila commenced soon after lunch, but not before a short tour of the city. Indeed, Ilocos Norte is a land of wonders.

The people, the place itself, and the distinct aura of oneness and solidarity. It was, for me, to be an experience that transcends the present world of turmoil, hatred, diversity and multiplicity.

For me, it was an eye-opener of sorts -- both spiritually and physically.

Dance of Light

I try to open my psychic senses to various people and places most of the time.

I would usually receive quick flashes of their personality or the general harmony of a place. I can easily find a spot where I will be more comfortable than in any other spot in the same locale.

A few months before the 4th of July, I became unusually attracted to the locality of Timog Avenue in Quezon City. I would often take this route every Saturday on my way to quest meeting points.

I have always taken the faster and relatively shorter route of Aurora Boulevard in the past, but passing through this longer route did not bother or stress me in any way.

Strange as it may seem, I simply liked the route and its crowded scenery.

But what perplexed me the most is the irrational feeling I've always felt when passing by this area where the former Ozone Discotheque used to be.

My pulse starts to beat faster and my body hairs would all stand up.

More often than not, my gaze gets directed at the upper balcony of its narrow facade. And for no apparent reason, I would just feel sad and interested, both at the same time. Whenever I pass through the bistro, the feeling of sadness intensifies then gradually fades away.

Many years have passed since that fateful night, but the agony of those who died in the fire still lingers in my mind.

I did not follow up on the Ozone Disco tragedy since it happened in March 18, 1996. The deprivation of justice for the victims of the fire, especially for those who died in the blaze, has somewhat made me keep my distance from the issue.

I wanted people to remember that eventful night and to learn from it. It was, after all, a learning experience for all of us.

Ironically for me, however, all I wanted to do was to forget the enormous feeling of pain and anguish felt by those who have become victims of such recklessness; more so for those whose spirits got "lost" in the tragic accident.

Guilt, love, regrets...

Young and energetic, the victims of the country's "worst tragedy in 50-years" could just not completely move on in the after life. Highly spirited and carefree, the young men and women who died chose to continue to be earth-bound. They wanted to see justice served, and bequeathed, upon their untimely death.

Guilt, love, regrets... even anger. Each one of them had a purpose for continuing to stay on with us.

Hair-raising unnatural occurrences have since become a part of this area at nightfall, all of which may be attributed to the listless spirits and victims who have chosen to remain earth-bound.

Soon after having regained their foothold, the surviving victims and relatives of those who perished formed a group known as the J.O.V (Justice for Ozone Victims). They help the relatives of the victims in every way they can.

In many instances, they have become instrumental in ensuring the progress of the case, from initial filing of the cases up to the actual hearing or trial. They also became invaluable partners in assisting the earthbound spirits so they could eventually move on.

The JOV has invited the Spirit Questors quite a number of times before, precisely with this particular goal in mind. Each time, more and more spirits got released from bondage and from their earthly attachments.

Today, out of an initial 162 people who have since perished in the fire, only 30 spirits remain unbound.

In the Spirit Questors' 4th (and possibly last) series of quests which was done on July 4, 1997, nothing special came about, except for the eventuality of events.

Coincidental about this quest was the fact that it is the fourth quest, done on the fourth day of the fourth month, immediately after the Ozone Disco tragedy's first anniversary.

Joining us for this quest are questors Perla, Geoffrey, Mindy, Macky, and Tracy. Members of the JOV and other concerned relatives of the victims have also joined us that day.

Together with Macky and Tracy, I decided to linger around the burnt foyer of the discotheque while waiting for the others to arrive.

Further down the hall, wide swinging doors open to a huge cavern of what seems to be the remains of the dance floor and its edifice.

With light coming from its destroyed ceiling, one can initially discern the area as a place of waste and havoc. One could also just imagine that underneath the debris and its sooth-covered floor, hundreds of human remains lie burned to ash and powder.

With every step we make, remnants of what used to be human lives crackle and crush unceasingly.

We decided to attune ourselves with the vibrations of the place.

In the least burnt portion of the foyer, Tracy, Macky and I formed a circle.

I sit facing the huge-panelled mirror, with the art-covered wall to my back. Macky sits facing the inner most door leading to the inside of the facade.

A few minutes after commencing, Tracy asked, "Do you hear that?" while simultaneously opening her eyes.

By then, we are already looking at each other hoping for an answer.

We carefully looked around and reassure ourselves that there is no other living person around -- except us, of course!

The Ozone Disco is completely sound-proof inside and out. Padded with sound proof-boards, the walls of the disco could easily prevent sound coming from the outside to be heard, and vice-versa.

Right then and there, we realized that the sound we were hearing could not have come from the outside.

Lub-dub. Lub-dub. Lub-dub. We could hear the sound again, slowly at first, before further intensifying. Audibly and a little louder than before, we can now hear the deep sounds of a beating heart, and it continued to puzzle us.

"What is it?" I asked.

Lub-dub. Lub-dub. The heartbeat continued.

Distinctively and much clearer this time, the sound appears to be originating from practically everywhere – from the walls, to the floor and to the ceiling. In fact, the sound seems to rebound from within the entire structure.

Lub-dub. Lub-dub. Lub-dub. Lub-dub...

The sound finally gives off a grave-deep quality and consistency.

Neither Tracy nor Macky could say a word. I re-focused my senses and instantly discerned something in my inner mind. I saw a giant, blood-red heart beating strongly and forcefully.

"Okay. Now I know," I told myself.

We stayed on for a while -- hoping to be one with the place, and to share in its sadness, anger, fright, and desolation. We then decided that we should all pray together.

We were then called to form our circles. Mindy, Melba (a parent of one of those who died in the fire), and I were asked to form one of the groups.

I was asked where I wanted to locate my group's circle so it could properly be logged. Instinctively and without any thought, I noted that I wanted to locate our circle in the upper foyer.

Then, as an afterthought, I asked myself why I wanted to position my circle in the upper floor. Surely, from my own experience, I will want to be in a place where the most number of dead bodies can be found.

Not wanting to allow my rational thoughts to affect the quests, I followed my third instinct.

On top of the winding staircase which leads to the manager's office at the second floor, everything seemed OK as if no fire has engulfed the area below.

The mini-bar is still intact, the chairs properly stacked on top of one another. The floorboards were neither ashen nor charred. The walls were also still clean except for some watermarks and dust.

The manager's office, on the other hand, is covered with grime and scattered pieces of paper. The upper foyer did not reveal any piece of evidence that a fire has claimed the lives of more that a hundred people there.

From the palisade that overlooks the entrance of the disco, a huge reinforced glass forms the inner and outer walls of the facade – and it showed no cracks or traces of being burnt.

A few candle residue and burnt papers on the floor and tables are also there, indirectly reminding the living of the untimely death of those who were in this place that dreadful night.

From the small window in the manager's office, one can establish a broad view of the dance floor which is so wide and dominating.

Somehow, I wondered if the one seated in that room on that fateful day could have had the chance to prevent what eventually became a tragedy, killing hundreds of young minds and potential achievers who were unable to escape the impending inferno.

Up until today, so many "what ifs" and similar other responsibilities are still left unanswered.

Before finally giving the go-signal to proceed with the quest, each of us is asked to light a candle in front of the glass wall.

Accompanied with prayers for the souls of the departed, the gesture is to symbolize our little offering. Afterwards, everyone joined hands and formed a circle to commence the Tower of Light.

Mindy suggested that we locate our circle in the ante-room of the second floor. Together with Melba, we pulled a round cocktail table at the centre, placing it in front of the bar.

We decided to remain standing since the chairs were all still stacked together.

Mindy then handed me a yellow, 4-inch candle to light. I lighted the candle and placed it in the centre of the table in front of us.

We held hands after that. At that point, I had my back turned to the glass wall fronting the building.

As I stood there facing the inner office overlooking the dance floor, I decided to take a quick glance at my immediate surroundings.

I was located at Mindy's right (the giving side) while Melba is to my receiving side. Together, we form a circle of three, the number of oneness.

We then closed our eyes and started to relax amidst the deafening silence.

"Is anybody here?" Mindy asked.
"I think so. I feel somebody at my right towards the rear," I said.

"Can you see the spirit?" Mindy followed up.

"I still don't see it," I answered

"Well, invite the spirit to the circle," Mindy urged.

"We have two spirits here with us, both female," I told the group.

With my eyes closed, I could discern two female figures.

I was certain they are female because of the unmistakably feminine curves and long hair. One of the spirits is standing while the other is seated on the floor with her knees folded onto her chest. She sat at the far corner of the room, her arms wrapped around her legs.

Then, all of a sudden, I felt an entirely new feeling. I felt light and free.

From where I was, I could see a vision of myself down below.

I see Mindy, Melba and myself holding hands in a circle of light. Then, just a few steps behind my physical body, I could see the elder of the two feminine figures trying to cautiously approach the circle.

I thought of moving closer to the figure, to simply encourage her to join the group in the circle. In an instant, I saw myself standing just a few inches beside her.

Without any form of communication, we looked at each other's eyes and she immediately understood that the circle meant no harm.

I held her left hand with my right hand then gently guided her into the circle. Her hand is smooth and soft. It bore no rough spots. She held onto my hand gently at first, then more firmly afterwards.

An unusual sensation then overwhelmed me. I was again standing beside Mindy in the circle. My right arm felt numb, and my hands were feeling extremely cold.

At that point, I can no longer discern whether Melba is still standing beside me or not. I simply ignored the logic of the mind, started to relax before continuing to attune myself to the situation, and to the

63

task at hand.

Again, beyond my closed physical eyes, I could see another being other than Melba standing to my right.

Then, I said, "I have one of them right here in the circle now."

I informed the group that the figure, who is a girl, is now standing beside me. It is curious of what we were doing.

I felt as if I occupied only half of my body, the right half completely unfelt and desensitized. Everything around me was dark and hazy.

Only the candle within the circle provided the illumination we need.

Then I heard a voice coming seemingly from nowhere.

"What is your name?" Mindy asked.

In an instance, the girl gently tagged at my right arm and moved closer. I looked straight into her eyes.

"Ja-s-min," she said without opening her lips.

"Jasmin," I repeated for the group to hear.

"How old are you?" Mindy asked further.

Jasmin then looked at me and smiled. She kept smiling and looking at me. Without breaking eye contact, I mentally asked Jasmin what her age was. She just continued to smile.

Then later on, she said, "Take a good guess."

"She will not tell. Approximately 18-20 years old," I said in response to Mindy's query.

"What are you still doing here?" Mindy countered.

I received no response from her.

Jasmin simply maintained her composure as if she heard nothing.

"Do you see any light?" Mindy again asked.

Slowly, Jasmin turned and looked outside the huge reinforced glass. She does not smile or express any form of satisfaction.

I could feel that her dominant emotion has completely turned from that of frightened, to sadness and loneliness. I followed her gaze. A foggy light glowed outside.

Jasmin looked solemnly into my eyes then gazed towards the light just outside the building, and then back to the reinforced glass.

"Yes, she can see it," I informed Mindy.

"Why have you not gone to the light?" Mindy seconded.

Tears slowly welled into the corner of Jasmin's eyes. She is tearful.

Gently, I asked her not to cry. I then assured her that we will help her. I also assured her of our support and assistance.

I then asked her mentally why she would not move on. She told me that she is trapped inside the disco. She could not go out and go on.

I was surprised at her answer.

I always thought that since their physical limitations have already been superseded by the loss of their body, spirits could go anywhere they please. Basically, they were already free spirits.

So I asked her why.

Slowly, Jasmin loosened her hold of my hand, went near the huge glass and pointed at it. Then, with a steady gaze, she told me that the glass facade is blocking her way.

Puzzled and bewildered at her reasoning, I told her that the glass could not, in any way, hinder her movement. But still she insisted.

Then, all of a sudden, I began to I understand.

Physically, the huge glass can definitely obstruct her movement. Jasmin still hasn't fully accepted her death and the freedom from limitations it offers. She has consciously perceived the glass as a barrier.

Gently, I took hold of Jasmin's fragile hands and softly squeezed them.

"Jasmin, you can pass through that glass if you want to," I softly told her.

"I could not pass through it," she said.

"You can. Just try," I encouraged her.

"But I'm afraid," she said.

"There is nothing to be afraid of. Just try," I further told her.

"But, I really am afraid," she begged, now almost tearful.

"I will be here. Just try. If you do not like it or if you suddenly feel afraid, just come back and I will be here waiting for you," I said.

"You will be here?" she asked.

"I'll be here. I will be looking after you. Just go on and try," I said.

Jasmin then slowly released her hold of my hand.

Slowly, she walked towards the huge glass. Then, she turned and looked at me.

"Go on, just try. You can pass through the glass," I beckoned her.

With a look of both fear and trust etched on her face, Jasmin slowly moved towards the glass.

Slowly, she extended her hand to touch it. Her hand passed through the glass. I could see the look of excitement and amazement on her face.

A smile eventually showed on her face. By this time, a third of her arm has already been extended through the glass. She walked away slowly, walking further and deeper down into the glass wall that has enslaved her all this time.

"Just go on and try," I said to Jasmin while mumbling to myself.

The foggy light I saw outside the reinforced glass facade gradually brightened and shined.

Jasmin's whole body is now almost completely outside the glass wall. Her figure floated cautiously towards the light source before gradually becoming smaller and smaller as she went deeper into the light.

Then, quite unexpectedly, she stopped and turned around.

"Just go on and try," I said, quite alarmed.

I was actually half-expecting Jasmin to come back and abandon her move to the light. Then her thoughts eventually spanned mine.

"You will be there, won't you?"

"I will be here," I said.

Jasmin then turned and continued on her way. The light eventually engulfed her totally until I could no longer see her.

"She is in the light now," I informed Mindy.

"Good," Mindy shot back.

I then became aware of Melba's hold on my right hand. She was there all along. I thought she broke the circle and left Mindy and I to quest alone.

"Now, call the other spirit," Mindy instructed.

With the light still burning brightly and steadily outside the glass wall, I tried to look for the other girl. I last saw her in the far corner of the room, seated on the floor.

Using the vision I had when I was still encouraging Jasmin to move on, I eventually found the girl. She is still on the same spot, seated on the floor by the far corner on the left side of the room facing the glass front.

She is now hysterical and panicky, obviously very afraid. I asked her to join us in the circle, but she refused. She is still in a state of shock and definitely afraid.

Suddenly, just as before, I saw the group and myself down below.

I was floating in mid-air, free and relaxed. I felt neither heaviness nor restrictions in my movements. I then saw the girl seated by the corner. She showed fear and hysteria. She clutched tightly onto her body while keeping her knees close to her chest and arms.

The circle of light is now just a few steps away from her. Mindy is holding my left hand, I was holding Melba's left, and Melba is also holding Mindy's left hand. Burning brightly at the centre of the circle is a half-consumed yellow candle, its soft drippings flowing on both sides.

I was leisurely watching the group when I suddenly heard a voice.

"Where is she?" Mindy asked.

"She is in the far corner of the room, very much afraid," I said.

From a state of weightlessness, I willed myself to be near the young girl. Instantaneously, I saw myself standing beside her. She is still crying.

As I sat beside her, I told the girl not to cry anymore and to be not afraid.

"I am a friend, I won't hurt you," I said to her softly.

"Are you Jasmin's friend?" I inquired.

She nodded as some sort of a response then continued shaking with fear and hysteria. Her hands began to tremble, and her mouth was jittering uncontrollably under her sigh. All the while, she maintained her position, seating tightly in the far corner of the room.

I offered my hand to her, saying, "I'm also a friend of Jasmin."

She soon mellowed then calmed down with what I said, but she did not take my hand. Instead, she looked at me straight in the eye.

"Ask her to join the circle," Mindy's voice again resounded from the circle.

"I don't think she wants to join us in the circle. She's very afraid," I told Mindy.

Then, turning to the girl, I asked, "Did you see what Jasmin did?"

Again, the girl nodded in response.

"What is your name?" Mindy asked.

At this point, the girl remained steadfast, so I offered my hand to her one more time.

She moved momentarily, but just as I thought she'd reach out for it, she immediately withdrew her hand.

I then took the initiative, saying, "I am also your friend. What is your name?"

In between sobs and shivers, she softly uttered her name.

"Anna."

By then, I was already holding her hand. I gently asked her to join us in the circle, assuring her that I will be her friend.

Anna's hand felt extremely cold. And just like Jasmin's, it is soft and smooth. She shivered in extreme coldness. I then guided her as she joined us in the circle.

Sensing that the only space available for her in the circle is my place, I guided her to my physical space. I then stood behind my physical body supporting Anna who is now in my place.

"Do you see the light?" Mindy asked.

Anna answered by looking at the bright light outside the glass wall.

"Do you want to go there, just like what Jasmin did?"

"I am afraid," Anna replied.

"Afraid of what?" asked Mindy.

"Mommy and Daddy," she said. Anna then started to cry once more.

"Do not be afraid of them, they will not be angry," Mindy reassured her.

Still, Anna continued to tremble and cry.

I was still standing behind Anna when I accidentally glanced at Melba.

Momentarily, I willed myself to be able to talk to Melba. I again became aware of my physical body.

"Anna," I began, "Melba is here with us. She is one of the parents of the victims who died here. As a parent, she will be able tell you that your mom and dad understands you and that they won't get angry," I explained, tears now welling in my eyes.

As a signal, I then gently squeezed Melba's hand, for her to say something. I again willed myself to leave and let Anna take over my place.

It took time for Melba to say something, but eventually she did.

"Anna," Melba began, "you might know me and I might know you. You did not want these things to happen to you, so your parents will surely not blame you for it."

Anna is still holding on to me at this point, listening intently amidst the unusual coldness of the place. As Anna's sobs became low and infrequent, I occasionally felt overwhelmed by the unfamiliar bone-deep coldness of the place.

"Like me, I lost a daughter," Melba continued her motherly advice. "But I never got angry at her because this is God's will."

As she spoke, I noticed that Melba's voice has started to waver and fluctuate. I looked at her momentarily and was not surprised to see her face glistening with tears.

By now, Melba is also crying. Tears flowed scantily at first from both her eyes. Then, as she continued, her tears began flowing freely.

Melba is still sobbing when she told Anna: "Go on my dear. Go towards the light. That is where you will find your friends and dearly beloved. You will understand everything when you get there."

Upon hearing this, Anna began to cry again. Her burst of emotion is unlike any other girl of her age. She cried and wailed furiously.

Before we know it, Anna has already broken the circle. She left the group and returned to the far corner of the room, seating opposite the huge glass wall.

With knees bent close to her chest and arms wrapped tightly around her, Anna started to cry again.

Surprised at her sudden reaction, I continued to watch Anna from afar. She looked at the light just outside the reinforced glass, then looked at me again. At that that instant, Anna caught a glimpse of my now teary eyes.

Before she broke her stare to bury her head in between her arms, she passed me her thoughts.

"I want to go to the light but," her thoughts trailed off. Still seated on the floor with her head in between her arms, Anna continued to cry and sob.

70

As I tried to ponder on my own thoughts while keeping my inner mind open to Anna's thoughts, I remained in the circle with Melba and Mindy.

Suddenly, from the back of my mind, I heard someone say, "I'm so afraid. Afraid, afraid, afraid…."

These words pushed itself in the forefront of my own thoughts.

"Anna wants to go to the light but she's afraid," I told Mindy.

"Right now, she is back in the corner, seated and crying," I added.

"Can we ask her to go to the light?" Mindy asked.

"She is afraid to even move again," I said.

"Anna, just go on. Go to the light now," Mindy urged her further.

Anna remained seated and unmoved. In between sobs, I could see her shiver and sigh. She just stayed there in the corner, sobbing. It seems no amount of prodding could move Anna out of that position.

"She is still in the corner," I informed the group a few minutes later.

The inert darkness and coldness of the place made Anna shiver and all the more frightened and scared of the unknown. Seeing Anna in that state made me think about my own fears.

When I see things others can not, my initial feeling is that of being lonely and cold. I also have this uncanny feeling of fearing death itself. When I think of death and the light beyond, my fear grows more and more.

These are just some of the things I initially feared about, and I now realize that Anna's fears are also my own.

Through psychic feeling, I can feel Anna's growing fear of the dark, the cold and the unknown.

As I lay there standing in the circle with Melba and Mindy, I felt my eyes begin to get cold and misty. I was so touched by Anna's lonely situation.

Her quandary is just but one among numerous other cases of souls whose situations have similarly become lost on them.

Today, I realized that Anna's feeling of loneliness and uncertainty also represents the pain, anguish and turmoil of other lost souls on earth. A pain that needs to be soothed, an anguish that needs to be calmed, a turmoil that needs to be arrayed, and a lost soul that needs to be guided.

The light behind Anna continued to shine. Notably, it pulsated as it glowed. It will brighten one moment and then dim in another.

The light now seems to be calling attention to itself; its radiance is now more expansive and wide.

"Since she will not move on by herself, we can try to call someone from the light to guide her," suggested Mindy.

"We can try," I shot back.

From the circle, we imagined a strong beam of light emanating from the centre of our foreheads. The light we envisioned is blue, and is about half an inch in diameter.

We focused the beam of light into the bright light beyond the huge reinforced glass then projected the beam of light so it will go deeper into the white light.

Slowly, the blue beam of light started changing to that of a dazzling white light.

I maintained my focus and concentration. After what seems to be an eternity, the bright light began to brighten and radiate. Slowly, its core shined and glowed.

By this time, the light has become so intense that it is now blinding and penetrating. Our blue beam of light is now engulfed and started to disappear within the now very luminescent light.

A figure then started to appear from within the light.

Anna continued to cry in the corner. She momentarily stopped when the light brightened and radiated past her. She looked into the light.

The figure from the light is now near Anna.
She is a lady dressed in a flowing, robe-like dress. Her dress-like covering blended well with the bright light around her. Her feet and her arms were not visible, but her hair flowed down freely. Her face radiated with a ghastly off-white colour.

Soon, Anna stopped crying.

For the first time, I saw a smile etched on her lips. Her eyes were sparkling, her face evoke a happy tone that's not flooded with tears and pain.

Anna's smile rippled through her face as she saw the lady from the light getting near her. At an arm's distance, the lady stopped beside Anna, momentarily standing still, before extending her hand to offer it to Anna. She then broke into a wide smile.

A picture of happiness is now clearly etched on Anna' face, and her excited movements showed it all. As she reached out for the hand of the lady from the light, it seemed as though Anna jumped as she stood.

Then, with just a single step towards the light, I saw Anna standing beside the lady from the light. Momentarily, Anna and the lady from the light looked back at us and into each other's eyes.

It seems that an exchange of thoughts has occurred. Then in a swift and gentle manner, they went back towards the light. They turned their backs on us as they slowly disappeared, hand in hand.

By this time, the light outside the huge reinforced glass facade has slowly dimmed. It then faded gradually. The glass facade no longer holds, enslaved and entrapped, two lost souls who got caught in a sudden change of existence – from that of living, to death.

I suddenly felt unusually heavy. My body felt anchored down. I felt utterly exhausted.

"This must be the feeling," I told myself. After the previous feeling of weightlessness, of unlimited boundaries and of being out of body, I seemed to be re-adjusting to the physical body.

As I opened my eyes, I saw a blurred vision of Mindy and Melba in front of me. Squinting and hoping to clear my sights, I soon became aware of the cause of these blurring.

Tears.

Tears welled in and around my eyes. I tried to think back. I could not remember crying during the quest, but I do remember seeing Anna as she cried and sobbed a lot.

After inconspicuously drying my eyes, I looked at Mindy and Melba. Both were also teary eyed, and were drying their eyes.

"Did you know that your whole right arm is shaking?" Melba asked.

"No. When did that happen?" I asked her, still baffled at the query.

"During the quest," Melba answered.

"Are you sure?" I asked, trying not to believe her.

"Yes, you were shaking a lot during the quest," seconded Mindy.

"But why are you 2 crying?" I asked them in return, hoping to steer the conversation away from me and my shaking.

"I haven't told you anything about myself or my family since we've only met today," Melba began saying while trying to hold back her tears. "I think I know who those 2 girls we just helped."

"Really? But how?" I asked Melba quite interestedly.

"I lost Gigi in the fire. My husband and I could not accept Gigi's untimely death. We refused to believe that she is dead. From the looks of it, Jasmin is Gigi's friend, Pia-Jasmin. Anna is also another friend named Jo-Anna. Both your descriptions of them correspond well to Gigi's friends as I knew them," confirms Melba.

"As I was talking to Anna, I felt as if I was talking to Gigi. Helping her to go and move on to the light has helped me, in return, to accept the death of my daughter and to believe in life after death. It also helped me free myself from holding on," Melba soon trailed off as she cried and sobbed uncontrollably.

As we descended the stairs down the foyer where everyone else was waiting, I paused and gazed at the huge 3-inch thick reinforced glass facade of the discotheque. Its lightly-tinted hue has trapped the mid-morning sunlight wanting to pass through.

In the same way that it trapped the sunlight, I now realized that the glass has also trapped 2 lost souls, Jasmin and Anna. Two lost souls wanting to move on but were instead barred, trapped and enslaved.

But then again, pondering on it some more, did the glass facade really trap the souls, or did it instead set them free?

No doubt about it, the huge reinforced glass facade has helped free Melba. It gave Melba a chance to understand, gifting her the freedom to understand fully the real meaning of unrestricted love. It helped set her free from the frightening bounds of her concept of "death," and from holding on to the memories of a dearly departed.

Our own quest experience also helped Melba understand that death is just the end of an old lease, and the beginning of a new life. The glass facade has given her some freedom -- a kind of freedom that was unsolicited but which, nonetheless, spontaneously evolved and presented itself during our quest.

As I looked at the discotheque one last time, I wondered how many more lost souls are still trapped in this burnt edifice. I could actually count them. Five, twenty, forty-five, sixty. For such a small place, that number seems to be quite a lot.

It also makes me wonder of the greater number who are still trapped in the living. Trapped in their own little world, trapped in a world of materialism, hate and selfishness, trapped in their own fantasies, and trapped in their own selves.

The huge glass facade of the discotheque has trapped two lost souls but eventually set them free. But more than that, it has also freed another, someone from the living, from her earthly bounds.

With tears in our eyes, we, the members of the Spirit Questors and myself, left the place where the "Dance of Light" began that fateful night in March.

Astral Drive

My initial attraction to the locality of Timog Avenue in Quezon City was actually uncalled for.

I did not know that a special quest will be scheduled for Ozone Disco until a few days later, when a request for volunteers was announced. Still, the thought never dawned upon me until I began writing about my profound and out-of this-world experiences.

My attraction to a certain place usually starts with unusual coincidences. It's either that I would suddenly get hold of the thought, and wherever I may be it would keep crossing my mind. Or I would be introduced to the place and next thing I know, I'm researching and learning more about it.

A few weeks prior to this unique quest, my level of attraction for nature became heightened. I would read books about nature, or watch a highly educating episode about nature in Discovery Channel. And sometimes, I would go out of the house and enjoy basking in the sunlight.

Oftentimes, I would feel sad and go sentimental over the declining state of the environment. I did not know that this unusual attraction for nature would actually mean something for me in the future. It could have been a preparatory attunement, premonition, or plain and simple coincidence.

Blue Bay Reefs in Palawan holds a number of mysteries and adventures under its sleeves. Its rich coral reefs and white sandy beaches can readily quench anyone's thirst for nature's best.

The vastness and exotic isolation of this particular place wills the heart to love nature back and be amazed at God's creations. The magnificence of Blue Bay Reefs' undersea world favours divers and lovers of the sea.

Its majestic caves and underwater structures, meanwhile, have not only enticed but also infinitely fascinated and captured every visitor's passion and desire to stay in this island paradise.

A day or two of vacation would have been such a short time to indulge in nature's beauty and elegance. It will surely break one's heart to leave the place unexplored. Furthermore, the richness of the sea allows it to claim its worthy title of being the world's best. It is truly a traveller's paradise, a home away from home.

Hidden behind this profound splendour and prosperity is a secret that the island has since become known for – an exotic primitiveness that's adored and loved by almost everyone who gets a chance to visit the place. But deep within its wild forests and thick undergrowth are mysteries still unexplained and unheard of.

People of every age who have grown up in the island often had one, nay, even two eerie experiences to share, and many of them opt to just keep it to themselves.

One of these well-kept, enigmatic stories is that of a local settler and her children who have been annoyed by unseen guests.

Mrs. GF, 40 years old, hails from another place other than Palawan.

She married and eventually decided to settle in Blue Bay Reefs where the years eventually caught up with her. Since her husband died in 1991, she has since raised on her own their 8 children, all of whom she dearly loves and cares for.

When they were still young, two of her children had already experienced unnatural occurrences; occurrences that have somehow sowed panic and fear. Only Mrs. GF's calmness and timely interventions has enabled her to save her children from further harm.

Upon the invitation of the agents who initially invited us for the quest, we went to Blue Bay Reefs to pay Mrs. GF a visit. We docked at a local town, and decided to pay a surprise visit to one of its senior residents, Aling Glo (*Aling* is a term of elderly respect in the local dialect). Upon our arrival at the pier, we found out that Aling Glo was already waiting for us.

It turns out that it was no surprise at all, as word has already been sent ahead of our visit.

Her Spanish-designed domain is located on the corner street of a road that leads to town, and another that leads to the beach. It looked more like a typical abode in the provinces with a balcony, capiz windows, and inter-locking wooden floorboards.

Way past the balcony, a 10-step stairs leads us to the receiving room and the main portions of the house. An old yet still sturdy rocking chair known locally as *tumba-tumba* sits silently on the balcony; apparently, it is still being used by its occupants to pass the time away.

Apart from the well-kept garden and frontage, the house is bordered by thick and overgrown shrubs and trees at the back and the sides. Inside, the house is adorned with a well-maintained wooden sofa and an *estante* (glass display). Inside the glass display are various oddities and souvenirs of the past generation. Clips, medals, small dolls, keys, necklace, and a lot more of other things.

Atop the glass escarpment, a 2-feet tall Japanese doll stands proud and tall. Aling Glo boasts that the doll was given to her by a Japanese soldier during the retreat of the Japanese Imperial Army.

While inside the house, I found the array of religious antics to be the most particularly attracting among all items therein. The statues, which ranged from the smallest, palm-sized Sto. Niños and other saints to the largest of its kind, practically occupied at least a fourth of the whole receiving area. Most are already decapitated and worn out, but suffice it to say, they are still well taken cared of.

Aling Glo tells us that these religious artefacts were either "saved" prior to being destroyed by the Japanese, or were unearthed in a mining process. These in turn, were handed over to her by the head miner and engineer.

Along with these religious statues were other age-old house wares, silver cutlery, terra cotta jugs and jars.

But what I found particularly interesting was the way the statues were being inhabited by an energy field, the source of which I could not fathom. The statues were, in a sense, very much alive and seemed to have a life all their own.

The moment I went near each one to examine them closely, I would feel a surge of energy flow through me. It was neither positive nor negative.

Though decapitated at most, the statues presented themselves as though they were a living part of the household. Much more, as one gets attuned to their particularly low vibrations, one would receive enormous amounts of information, such as its background and storied past.

But as Aling Glo recounts, these were not the reasons behind the family's unique experiences.

Pedro Junior, aptly nicknamed Junior, was about 8 years old when his odd experiences first began.

One particular night, at around 11:30, Aling Glo heard footsteps of people walking up and down the wooden floorboards. Under pressure, the boards would creak slightly, so Aling Glo was sure somebody (*or something!*) had been walking up and down the stairs. She would later find out that no one among her household was up and about during that time.

Her nightly visitors will continue their nightly visits for some time. She will hear them walking audibly on the receiving room from the stairs fading away as it passed her room. After a few nights, a shrill, high pitched and soft whistle would now precede her nightly social calls.

The whistle would often begin from the darkened backyard, slowly ascend to the closed front door by the front porch then continue along the sitting room. However, it would slowly fade away before long.

At first, Aling Glo got neither bothered nor alarmed at the nightly visits as she eventually got accustomed to these occurrences.

That is, until one night, when a sudden scream was heard from one of the adjoining rooms. It was already in the middle of the night when she heard her son Junior, shout for help.

Hastily rushing out of her room to look at Junior in the other room, Aling Glo was taken aback to see Junior in a terrible state of fright and terror.

He was tucked up in bed and was perspiring very heavily. His blanket was rolled up to his face as he trembled uncontrollably.

A caring mother would do everything to console her son, so Aling Glo slowly and cautiously went up to Junior to reassure him that nothing is wrong and that she would be there for him.

A child in her mother's arms will definitely take the fear away from any child.

When asked what made him so frightened, Junior narrated to his mom a rather unusual encounter. A few nights back, Junior said, he suddenly had this feeling that there is another person who would join him in his room.

It would often come in at night, and a short but high-pitched whistle will usually precede it. Soon after, he would feel the same presence moving about his room.

Peculiarly, the unseen guests did not bother him at all – at first. Junior sensed that it meant him no harm. Not until that night when his unseen friends started becoming violent and too aggressive for him to handle.

Puzzled at this revelation, Aling Glo sought to qualify his son's statement. What was he seeing? Who are they? What did they want?

Junior explained that at first, he saw nothing more than just silhouettes. Shadows of perplexed colours and sizes. Then recently, it started to take a more precise form and shape.

At its peak manifestation, it revealed itself as a creature of about two to three-feet tall, with fairly-coloured complexion and funny looking hat and boots. Its eyes are vertically oriented and are fiery red in colour. Its upper lip had no groove.

Most of what Junior was seeing is akin to small humans, except for some features. Some were really friendly-looking, while the others had beards and looked very old.

Mischievous dwarves

These small creatures of the underworld are obviously fond of Junior. For one reason or another, they had favoured him as a friend. Yet for Junior, their fondness of him exceeded his human comprehension.

On this particular night, these entities of small stature have exceedingly turned violent and destructive. They have started to become rough and rude in terms of their games with Junior. They started to jump, hop and skip on him. They were literally pounding and hurting him, and he was getting tormented and maltreated.

While the others enjoyed themselves jumping onto Junior, the others are having a good time strangling him. Unknowingly, they were asphyxiating him to death and that is when Junior started to shout for help.

Aling Glo stayed with Junior for quite some time until after things started to settle down again. She would stay awake at night and stand guard at Junior's bedroom door. She would stay in her *tumba-tumba* until the wee hours of the morning and rock herself to sleep.

As days went on, she eventually decided to pass the night away inside her own room. She would still hear the floor wobble and creak each night, yet no similar incident had happened to Junior ever since.

Not until one night when she got awakened by the sound of feeding bottles knocking onto each other. She was sure that she had organized Junior's feeding bottles in their proper places the night before.

However, it is now quite audible that the feeding bottles are banging unto each other. She opted to ignore the manifestation.

The following night, instead of feeding bottles banging onto each other in the adjacent room, the plastic bags beside Aling Glo started to creak and crumple. Aling Glo was so scared that she did not even bother to look at the manifestation happening beside her.

She instead closed her eyes and pretended not to see or hear anything. Eventually, she fell asleep.

A few days have passed without any more disturbances. Aling Glo is quite relieved that the strange occurrences that have been haunting her family have stopped. She is wrong, however.

One night, she brought Junior into her bedroom for the night. Making sure that the mosquito net edges were folded underneath the mattress to protect them, she began to sing a lullaby for Junior, until both of them fell asleep.

In the middle of the night, however, a familiar short, high-pitched whistle awakened Aling Glo. Following the origins of that shrill sound, and amidst the creaking of the floorboards, she eventually heard footsteps.

Then the familiar coldness of the atmosphere started to overwhelm her.

Her body hairs started to stand and she felt her head beginning to swell. Then, the edges of the tightly tucked-in mosquito net began to move and float in the air.

As quickly as she could, Aling Glo said a round of prayers. The mosquito net fell limply on the side and then the manifestations stopped.

The manifestations eventually became infrequent, prompting Aling Glo to believe that all these will stop in due time. However a few weeks since the last manifestation, Junior's cry for help once again alarmed Aling Glo.

This time she found Junior much more terrified than before and totally afraid. In between sobs, Junior told his mother that a huge face suddenly appeared from the ceiling. The face forced its way out of the ceiling, and in doing so, its features eventually got distorted.

According to Junior, its face neither belonged to a man or a woman. Soon after, the face from the ceiling appeared in front of him. At the foot of his bed, he saw a medium-built lady of fine qualities. She is dressed in multi-colour fabric, is fair-complexioned, and has vertically-oriented eyes that were fiery red in colour.

Numerous subordinates also accompanied the being, and they were all around his room. The dwarves told Junior that the lady is their Queen. The queen was looking leisurely but steadily at Junior when he began to panic, and shouted for help.

Terrified and bewildered at these occurrences, Aling Glo stayed awake the whole night that day, praying for Junior's safety.

Immediately the following day, Aling Glo looked for Maning Dante, who had just arrived from Northern Luzon. Generally, people from Northern Luzon are considered natural shamans, healers and psychics.
When Aling Glo learned of his successful control of unnatural occurrences in the past, she thought that she could consult him about his son's nightly "visitors." Maning consented, and was soon in Aling Glo's place.

Maning Dante is known in his barrio as an local *Albulario* (faith healer). He is also the most respected among his peers, and is reputed to be the best. He moved to Luzon a few years ago because he wanted to be with his family. Now, the old man has moved backed to Blue Bay Reefs for some reason.

Immediately after stepping into Aling Glo's front porch, Maning's body hairs stood up. He instantly felt an unusual level of energy and presence within the household.

Right then and there, he informed the family that an earth elemental has been disturbing them, specifically dwarfs of the mischievous type. Maning decided to cast a healing spell at Junior. Before the actual casting of spell, Maning temporarily lent a small talisman for Junior to use. It was a small metallic bronze object from Luzon given to Maning by a friend who had a dwarf for a friend.

Maning then placed the amulet on Junior's chest. The amulet, which had the figures of both an angel and the devil engraved on it, is oddly shaped and contained an inscription in Latin. The boy, who was peculiarly cold to touch before the amulet was placed on his chest, began to feel warm and energized again.

Maning explained that Junior is cold to the touch because the dwarfs are all over him, virtually covering him and becoming very much attached to the boy. When Maning placed the amulet on Junior, the dwarfs scampered off and began to detach themselves from the boy.

The next few days went by without any further incidences.

A healing ritual

After having prepared himself for the planned healing ritual to be done on Junior, Maning commenced. First and foremost, he asked Aling Glo to find a few things he will need in the process: a large crab's claw; a black palay (rice seed); a set of cobwebs specifically found under the hut; some coal ashes and a coconut shell.

Maning began the healing ritual by hanging the crab's claw at the door's upper wooden frame. He said that this would help repel unwanted spirits and elements. He then covered Junior with a white blanket.

Maning then carefully and ritually placed the ashes and the burning coal in the coconut shell, passing on this smoke-producing implement around Junior's chakra three times. With the smoke it produced, Maning was able to discern the cause of all these disturbances.

A few months back, Junior used to play at the backyard. He often played with Charlie, his older brother. During one of the games that they played, Junior climbed a huge Guava (*Psidium guajava)* tree unwary of the perils it could bring.

Unfortunately, a dwarf kingdom has inhabited the guava tree and Junior's leisurely climb has caused the dwarves to like him. They have since been playing around with him.

Prior to Maning's arrival, another local *albulario* has also advised Aling Glo to have Junior treated by a "faith healer" since he suspected that Junior's disturbances were caused by dwarfs.

Aling Glo however, ignored the advice, hoping instead that the dwarves would not hurt his sons. Charlie heard the suggestion of the *albulario* and, in a fit of anger, went up to the mountains to curse the dwarves.

Upon returning home that night, everybody was surprised to see Charlie black and blue, as if he had been mugged. His lower mouth and jaw were also bruised very badly. But despite the bruises, he did not feel any pain.

Maning added that had Aling Glo not been prompt enough to call him to do the ritual, she would have lost Junior to the lure of the unseen.

During the ritual, Junior would actually stiffen every time someone came close to him.

After the ritual, Maning asked Junior to rest in bed and try to recuperate. He also instructed Aling Glo to do a healing water ritual that he prepared especially for her.

Using a large kettle to boil some leaves, Maning then concocted a magical potion which he asked Aling Glo to use daily in Junior's bath. He advised her to always retain a small amount of the original water in the kettle and to just add new water accordingly.

He said that the new set of water would always be partly contaminated by the original "magical water," making it just as potent as before.

One day while Aling Glo is getting ready to bathe Junior, the pail of water that she prepared containing Maning's healing potion suddenly overturned and got splashed on the floor.

Luckily, she still had some extra healing water so she just boiled it again and refilled the pail with a new set of water. She then went to Junior's room to fetch the boy.

When she returned, she was surprised to see the second pail of water again overturned and almost empty. She managed to save a small amount from the overturned pail which she used to make another set. She again filled the pail with water then held onto it more carefully this time. After which, she was able to bathe Junior without any more disturbances.

After Maning's healing intervention on Junior, their nightly visitors did not show up anymore. Well, not until after Junior turned forty years old.

Having missed home and his parents, Junior, now the local distributor of sweetened cashew nuts, went back to Blue Bay Reefs for a short vacation. His stay in the province was uneventful and relatively peaceful.

He had hoped to savour the province's fresh air and to enjoy once again the rich coral reefs of the undersea world. The scenery gave him a break from the hustle and bustle of life in Manila. It gave him a chance to relax and spend some bonding time with his family and loved ones.

On his last day in town, Junior planned to take the earliest boat ride to Manila. The early morning boat trip to Manila was scheduled to leave at around 2 a.m. Aling Glo had stayed awake all night, preparing Junior's things and other belongings. She even prepared him some freshly cooked sweetened cashew nut for his snack and 'pasalubong'.

As 2 a.m. neared Aling Glo heard a faint whistle from outside of the hut. She ignored it at first, thinking it was just towns mate passing through. However, when her body hairs started to stand on its ends and her head began to swell, Aling Glo was overcome with fear.

A sudden feeling of coldness overcame her. Again, she heard a short yet high-pitched whistle. Suddenly the shrill sound that has become all-too familiar to Aling Glo echoed through the hut once more.

It first seemed to come from the outside, then as instantaneously as it came, the sound was now inside the hut. The sound moved around the house until it came to a familiar spot – Junior's bedroom.

At this point and for some unknown reason, Aling Glo began to tremble.

Junior hurried out of his room obviously wary of the sound. He stopped for a brief moment then looked reassuringly at his mother. Right then and there, it stopped. Nothing can now be heard except absolute tranquillity.

It was almost two o'clock in the morning. Junior gave Aling Glo a loving, heart-felt embrace. Aling Glo hugged her son back and gave him some motherly advice.

As Junior bade goodbye and was about to leave the family domain, again the short high-pitched whistle is heard once more. Clearly etched on Aling Glo's face is her motherly concern. She now remembers the days when she almost lost Junior to the dwarves. A loss not any parent could take. A loss that could leave a void and emptiness and which definitely no one can fill.

Now, as Junior walks past the bamboo gates to the nearby Blue Bay Reefs pier, the shrill sound of an unseen companion slowly fades away with him as well.

As Junior casually walks away, the short, high-pitched whistle fades away as well to a place where Aling Glo could just as well lose her son – this time, to the sheer lure of the city lights, a temptation of the unseen and unnatural. It turns out that the sound was meant as a final goodbye.

Junior is now ready to leave. Aling Glo wonders when her son would be back – to refresh himself again with the beautiful yet mysterious secrets of Blue Bay Reefs.

These age-old stories considered myths and fables at Blue Bay Reefs have grown and have somehow been a part of the local belief. But what most local inhabitants and settlers do not know is that such paranormal stories actually exist.

Little do they know that more hair-raising events had happened within the locality in the recent past. With only a few people knowledgeable of these ghostly occurrences, such stories have been kept a secret from the public which has grown pessimistic and sceptic of these narratives.

But more than just perceptions, various interests are also being protected and cared for.

Coral Cove: a journey to the other side

Blue Bay Reefs prides itself with its world class resorts and virgin waters. Situated at the southern most part of the island of Luzon, the island itself boasts of various underwater caves and rivers, pre-civilization tribes, burial caves, and other fascinating natural structures.

The Blue Bay Reefs group of islands is home to the world's best beach resorts. Mini islands within the area provide the traveller the best there is: Coral Cove, Reefer, Paradise, and whole a lot more. Each island has its own unique secrets and mysteries.

Tracing back to its pre-development years, these islands have evolved into a complex combination of extraordinary beauty and romance coupled with bizarre and paradoxical simplicity.

Coral Cove island resort is the second to be developed. Stationed halfway between Paradise, its forebears, and Reefer, its paragon, Coral Cove pleasures itself with its proximity to the natural wonders of the earth.

The small and big lagoon, the Virgin caves, the astounding coral reefs and the marvellous sea creatures it cradles are all located within Coral Cove's dominion.

From the Northeast, Coral Cove is a pygmy if compared to the expansive brine of mother earth. Entrusting its rear to the high cliffs and mountains of the island, the resort is actually hidden away from the open sea.

Although constrained in a shallow bay area, the island is actually a beauty to behold. Its surrounding waters are clear, pristine and un-spoiled by human intervention.

Pampered to its impulses, its rich marine resources have become people-friendly. Only the deep waters of the South China Sea hold the remnants of its storied past and other unexplored mysteries. Its deep-blue to moss-green reflective waters add terror to what it might deliver from within.

Detached from any form of human association, no one would ever know the truth behind the mysteries of Coral Cove. At night, when the stars are out, the island transforms into a haven of sorts: a resort for the traveller, a sanctuary for lost souls, a shelter for the wanderer, a refuge in the night and a place to promenade for its natural native dwellers, the unseen.

Coral Cove Island was soon able to harbour temporal settlers coming from the mainland. Most of the emigrants are workers at the resort. Apart from the travellers, early migrants also took a liking to the place and somehow made efforts to permanently acclaim the place. In time, both indigenous people and immigrants intermingled with each other.

Tristan was one of the early settlers in the place. He worked at Coral Cove as a dive master. As guests become enthralled to take a glimpse of the wondrous beauty of the undersea, Tristan is the one who accompany them.

Tristan routinely ushers observers to this infrequent sojourn. Tristan loved the sea so much that he decided to permanently live at Coral Cove Island. Needless to say, he fell in love with the island. And this love would not go unanswered.

On a dark moonless night, when the great sea turned to a raging force of endless mist, Tristan was offered a kind of love unheard of in this world.

While all alone in his house located in the high cliffs and the untouched forests of Coral Cove, a cold breeze suddenly put a damp sensation on his tanned complexion.

Tristan felt an eerie feeling of another presence inside his room. As the high seas continued its own crescendo, his head began to swell, his ears started to feel extremely cold and icy. All these had happened amidst the comfortable confines of his quarters.

From the dark shadows of the resort, a figure began to emerge. From out of the shadows, the figure of a lady began to form – gradually at first, until it became more pronounced.

Just as the ocean overflows to the shore, as free-flowing as the frenzied waves that splashed on the breakwater, a lady dressed in flowing apparel soon appeared. Her gentle radiance contrasted with the blackness of the night.

Standing quietly in the corner of his room, Tristan could feel the overflow of emotions from this fair lady. A nymph-like creation was standing before Tristan at this very moment.

Overwhelmed by the vision, Tristan could utter nothing but prayer. Oh, how he wished that the apparition before him would disappear! Outside, the ocean whitecap resounds endlessly while the sea continues to spray its mists amid the growing coldness of the night.

Suddenly, a surge of light beamed into Tristan's puffy eyes. The night is over. Warm sunlight soon radiated into a glorious and cosy feeling around him.

With nary a trace of the previous night's occurrence, Tristan felt energized and refreshed. However, Tristan also felt an unnatural attraction for the mountains.

Although Tristan still feels his innate passion for the sea and its treasures, the day went on with him being consciously hounded by the surrounding mountain. He has now become much more aware of its mighty presence and monumental prominence. He longed to find out what sort of secret or mystery lay deep within its recesses.

And just as the sea has held some dark, hidden and unknown knowledge, Tristan wondered if the mountain could also reveal as much as the ocean floor would. Night came about quickly. The day is over for Tristan.

He prepared for the coming new day not knowing that the night was just about to begin.

Tristan woke up to a familiar coldness around him. He could feel a strong presence within his room. Then just as in the night before, his body hairs started standing on its ends. He again felt extremely cold and chilly while his ears grew cold and icy as the ocean waters are at night. He shivered in bed.

From out of the corner of his eyes, Tristan again perceived a being slowly appearing from the far corner of the room. He could discern a shadowy figure amidst the brightly turned on light. Much to his amazement, the figure resembled exactly the same apparition he saw the other night. However, it has become more pronounced. He is now facing a fairy.

A few years later after that terrifying night, a new set of developers soon leased the whole chain of island resort. Paul and George, the new owners, wanted only the best for Blue Bay Reefs.

They carefully studied the preservation and conservation of its natural environment and out of their passion for the environment they have been awarded numerous recognitions for their efforts. Blue Bay Reefs remains to be the best there is. Its reputation goes around the world for its unique and exciting offerings.

Barely touched and disturbed, Coral Cove retained its original beauty and splendour. Its mysteries and secrets remain unearthed. It remained naive to those who have come and gone.

Well, not until recently.

One night, when the moon was out and the ocean turned roughly on its great belly, a guest was heard shouting in terror and panic in one of the cottages. Employees of the resort rushed out to the frightened guest and offered him assistance. Puzzled at the circumstances of the incident, the staff queried the guest what happened.

The guest narrated that while peering out of his window, he suddenly saw a luminescent form appear. The ethereal glow of the florescent light and contrasting darkness of the twilight amplified the spectre form.

Prior to that, the guest said that had an eerie feeling that someone was watching him. The hair on his nape stood up, his ears started to feel icy cold, and all his body hairs started standing on its ends.

When he looked out of the window, the phantom figure was gone.

Nothing unusual happened in the succeeding days. Everybody soon forgot the ghostly incident.

One late night, Gerry was asked to close the front office reception. The wind blew lightly and the seawater sprayed salty mists over the land. At the pier, the lone guard watched the flickering lights from a distance. No amount of light could brighten the dark and lucid waters fronting Coral Cove. The endless swishing of water on the rocky breakwater mesmerizes the unwary listener to the lure of its opulence.

Having turned off all the lights, Gerry made a second round of check on the door locks. As he turned to leave, Gerry caught a glimpse of a pale ghostly vision inside the souvenir shop. Unsure of what he saw, Gerry re-focused his sight more intently. After doing so, his head distended to a feeling of disproportion, and his arms went cold and chilly.

Gerry's stomach churned and his legs started to turn into gel. He could barely stand up. A mixed feeling of fright and amazement played inside his head. Gerry could clearly see what frightened him – a luminescent 'white lady'.

Not wanting to wait for the situation to get worst, the owners, Paul and George, called on the Spirit Questors. Taking advantage of the holiday break and the availability of the members, Paul scheduled for a quest at Coral Cove Island on April 7, 1998.

As advised by Paul, the boat ride to Coral Cove would last for about one hour and a half from the Blue Bay Reefs airstrip.

Had I not been a part of this group that travelled to Blue Bay Reefs to investigate the mysterious phenomenon, I would not have altogether believed the stories. Amidst the grandeur, splendour and magnificent beauty of the place lies hidden secrets and unseen beauty.

Left out of the morning plane ride to the island because of some logistical problems (as what usually happens in out-of-town quests), Gary L. and I got booked in the afternoon flight. As the plane took its ascent, I again felt awed and tongue-tied by the unfolding beauty below.

Nature's glory and magnificence showed itself to me once again as I took a comprehensive view of Mother Earth. Indeed, life as I was accustomed to it is just a part of a bigger and larger system. The simple beauty that I so greatly adore is now just a speck of a far greater beauty.

By mid-afternoon, the plane landed in the local airport. Dust turned up as the dirt-levelled runway welcomed us. Lined on both sides of the airport are trees and wild grass.

While the plane taxied onto the tarmac, I noticed a small portion of the clearing by the side of the runway. It was obviously cleared and made for a certain purpose. I just would not know what. However, though my psychic senses were turned off, I got the impression of something huge and animal-like that was within the clearing.

I even got the impression that this something was racing with the plane as we taxied. I ignored these images, telling myself that this should not concern me at all.

The boat ride took us about an hour or so before we reached Coral Cove. By sunset, we have reached the small island. Strategically located within a bay, the resort would not be visible from the open seas. It is also protected from strong winds and waves which could otherwise decapitate the elegant and restful structures within.

As we prepared to disembark, I took a few minutes to scan the area. The mountain and thick foliage by the resort's rear gave me the impression of elementals – elementals of various forms which abound in the area.

The now calm waters of the South China Sea likewise sent shivers down my spine and nape. Something that is so unusual about the deep waters kept bothering me. This is the first time that I felt that way. I am usually not afraid of any form of bodies of water. This time however, I knew that something is amiss.

As Gary and I settled into the reception area, I sensed a presence which immediately retreated into the mountains. Like before, I just ignored it.

The courteous and very accommodating staff informed us that the group went to Paradise Island to check out on something. Obviously, the hotel's staff was not informed of the nature and purpose of our visit.

While Gary settled and unpacked, I took a moment to promenade around the place and feel the energies present. It is now past seven o'clock in the evening.

Established in the middle of nowhere and with the whole resort powered by generators, darkness soon began to settle everywhere.

I first strolled into the water cottages and saw nothing unusual. Then I roamed around the mountain cottages. With fine cold sand swallowing up my every step, I suddenly felt the minute hairs by my arm stand. I found myself in the shadows of the resort's water centre. I continued walking towards the other cottages. As I neared the base of the bell tower, the cold sensation I was feeling became stronger and more intense. My head started to feel cold as the other parts of my body did. There was no wind or breeze to put the blame on this phenomenon, and everything was so quiet and still.

I went closer to the thickened foliage of trees and wild plants. As I did so, the feeling within me intensified further. My body felt cold so I rubbed my palms on my arms to generate heat. However, a unique feeling of swelling-cold crept within my body and I felt cold from within.

The rest of the group arrived just in time as buffet dinner is being served. We savoured the sumptuous food while re-living the episodes in some of our quests.

A quest on top of the mountain

The order of the day was finally given. We were to conduct a quest from within the mountain-top of Reefer Island – a quest that would somehow prove even us would not be spared from the unearthly feelings offered by those from the other side.

We relaxed for a while after dinner, pampering ourselves with a romantic interlude of being under the stars at night, in an open beach and far away from the fast-paced life of technology and science.

Nevertheless, unknown to the rest of the guests and staff, we were simply passing time away until such time that most would be asleep and it will be late at night. Then we can start the quest deep into the night as planned.

As time passed, I got puzzled by the scarcity of unseen presence within the premises of the resort. Most of the unseen presence are either on the forest or on mountainsides. None would stay long on the resort's confines.

A group of young questors located their circle by the resort's lounge. Prior to the circle, the group performed the Tower of Light. After 20 minutes of the Tower of Light, the circle re-located. Tony facilitated that group while the others assumed their responsibilities as the primary channels.

"Is it here?" Tony asked.

"Yes," came the reply.

Tony did a round of greeting to the enchantress.

"Good evening. We are a group of psychics called the Spirit Questors. We know that you know about us because you talk about us just as we talk about you. We are here not to banish, but we are here to help mediate and come to terms with those who lives here," Tony began.

The fairy did not directly respond to Tony's greeting but instead conveyed a message, a message which I deciphered to mean something like "... the fairy had loved before. She fell in love with a man who turned down her offer. She grieved over the pain but eventually got over it. She fell in love again..."

The fairy's offer of love can now be fully understood by those whom she offered it to. Often, it would push the object of her affection away. Tony explained to the fairy that such a love could never work out right. She belongs to another world while "...we belong to another."

"Why are you showing yourself to others?" Tony followed-up.

"...I want to show myself to others because no one gave attention," she said.

"Please do not show yourself because it scares the guest and staff away," Tony pleaded.

"I will," she replied rather sadly.

"Is there anything you like to ask or be done?"

"A wind chime over by the coconut tree in the middle of the beach," she answered.

"It will be done," Tony assured her. "Is there anything more?"

"There is ..." one of the secondary channels followed-up. "...a small tree house of sort," I seconded. "... right in the middlemost coconut tree by the beach."

"The wind gets pretty strong especially when there's a strong storm, don't you think it would be hazardous?" asked Paul.

"Just a small, tiny tree house will do," Gary countered.

"There is a wind chime in the shape of a house available locally," another questor added.

"We will let the owners of the place know of your requests," Tony uttered.

"Were you the same creature who appeared by the water cottages a few years back?" I asked?

"No," she replied.

Following her answer, an entirely new vision flashed across each and everyone's inner mind.

A vision of the dark and mysterious waters of the South China Sea, a view of a subterranean system of existence and a blurred but perceptible scene out of an entirely different group of beings.

A waft of cold wind then gently blew. It raised the hair on everybody's nape and arms. A sudden sensation of not being alone overwhelmed the group. The Spirit Questors then affirmed of the vision.

Everybody heightened his or her awareness and perception to an extent.

"Thank you very much for talking to us. We will pass on your message to the owners of the place," Tony said to the fairy while starting to close the circle with everyone saying a short note of thanks.

The next day, the sun woke us up with an uncanny display of brightness and brilliance. The sun reflected its mighty rays off the sparkling waters of the South China Sea, and waves splashed endlessly at the breakwater.

In the background, Gary's choice of music played softly on his portable disk player. After a heavy breakfast of choice fruits and native Filipino dishes, our group of eager young questors gathered at the resort's lounge for the last in a series of three quests.

Everyone anticipated the quest as it was believed to be the most exciting and thrill-filled. As we were about to go, Paul asked everyone to secure for ourselves a pair of diving shoes from the water centre. He reminded that we will desperately need the slip-free soles and the tough rubberized material of the shoes. He added that the shoes would provide us much greater safety in this particular quest.

We piled into 2 motorized boats and when everyone was already onboard, the motorized boats relentlessly cut through oncoming waves. The waves are now quite high as the wind blew stronger from the East. Occasionally, the boats would fly above the water and land with a big splash just a few meters ahead.

Not taking the risk of being thrown overboard, everyone held on tight to the boat for dear life. After about 30 minutes of an exhilarating and thrill-filled boat ride, the dinghy slowed down near a huge outcrop of rocks in the middle of the sea. No beach could be seen anywhere.

"Are we there yet?" Gary asked.

I saw a grin etched slowly on the boatman's face. He then asked each one of us to lie down on the boat's floor as low as possible. While instructing us to do so, he manoeuvred the boat's bow towards a small opening in the rocks. As he did so, the boat then entered an opening barely the size of the dinghy.

Once inside, a huge darkened cavern slowly revealed itself to us. The boatman then passed on a few searchlights which we all gladly turned on.

The cavern's enormity and vastness swallowed the torch's frail light.

Gently, the boatman guided the dinghy deeper into the chambers far inside the cave. Pitch black darkness is now all around us. The only light that filtered from the outside is a small opening through which we came through but it is now a few meters behind us.

Water splashed on the cavern's jagged-edges. The air is heavy and stale.

As the boat came to a stop at the far side of the cave, we all began to pile out slowly and carefully.

One of the boatmen went ahead and lit candles along the inclined and uneven path walk. Rocks of all sizes and shapes extended out of our way. The rocks are slippery and knife-sharp. The tough rubberised shoes protected us from any possible danger.

A small clearing presented itself at the end of the pathway. Extending to the right on a perilous edge, a statue of the Lady of Lourdes immaculately stood still. Candle waxes lay melted on the base.

Down below, seawater continued to splash and swoosh on the rocky edges. Farther up the dangerously inclined pathway, which gradually joins the ceiling, I sensed a presence that seems to be patiently looking down at us.

As the questors positioned themselves, Tony instructed everyone to form the Circle, making sure that everybody is positioned and psychically well balanced. We commenced the quest proper.

Paul sat on my left while Tony instructed George to sit on my right.

The rest of the group is strategically placed to balance the energies. My back is towards the statue of the Virgin Mary and beyond her, the minute opening to the second chamber of caves.

A few years back three seasoned divers drowned in the lower limits of the second chamber. Their bodies were not recovered until after three days later. The mystery behind their deaths is the apparent disappearance of their bodies in the same area where they drowned.

Search and Rescue teams are very sure they have searched the area very thoroughly back and forth. However on the third day the bodies were found at the same spot.

I closed my eyes trying to concentrate on the thoughts of the three divers who have drowned. Three candles are lighted and placed inside the circle. While the candles illuminated the place, all I could see inside my mind is darkness. I felt extremely cold and chilly. My breathing was deep and heavy. I felt suffocated. I started to perspire despite the cold chill inside me. I felt three other presences within us.

A female was standing behind me and two males were positioned across me on both sides. They were just standing and observing us. Then the all familiar splashing of seawater on the rocky-edges started to faint. I felt my ears fill with pressure.

The next sound I heard are bubbles popping. A flash of light suddenly caught my attention. Next to the bubbles I can hear Tony's voice.

"I want you to do astral travel," I heard him say. "Go back to the moment before their death."

These are the accounts of what I have psychically seen during the time that Tony instructed and guided me to re-count the events. These events revealed itself through me from the eyes of one of the divers. It is as if I am looking at things from her point of view. As if I am her and she is me.

> I am swimming in a small and dark tunnel. Together with me are seven other divers. Our dive master led the way down the claustrophobic tunnel towards the second chamber. The angle of descent is steep and the crawl way twisted towards the left.

> As we dove deeper, the person in front of me stopped at an opening towards the right. The tunnel on the right is relatively perpendicular to the main tunnel.

He signalled for us to explore the tunnel. We broke away from the main group. I followed him whilst another male friend followed me. We followed the tunnel for about a few hundred yards. The lead diver's flashlight is insufficient to light the very dark tunnel as the torch of the last man did.

Gradually the tunnel narrowed in. Sensing of the empty adventure to which we have waylaid, I signalled the lead man for us to turn back and re-join the main group. In addition I got a glimpse of my air gauge to which I am running low.

Taking our cue, the lead man turned around. I signalled the last man to do same and our order of entry is now reversed. The last man is now our first man and the previous first man is now last. A few seconds after the turnaround, the last man started to push me from behind.

He wanted us to go faster which we cannot lest we disturb the seabed. In his haste he tried to overtake me as well as the lead man. The cramped tunnel cannot accommodate us. A struggle ensued.

In the process, the dust covered seabed stirred up, obstructing everything. Visibility is now zero. The flashlight fell into the black abyss. Darkness. Panic overwhelmed me. My sense of direction is lost. My breathing is now heavy and laboured.

In the dark I lay alone, cold and quiet. The darkness alone comforts me. It helps me forget the pain and the thought of dying. In the dark my senses are decreased. Slowly, however, I felt an increasing pressure in my ears.

My chest feels tight and dull. My eyes started to feel heavy. I feel sleepy. My hands and feet are numb. They feel heavy and almost not a part of me. Then slowly against my will I closed my eyes. Still darkness surrounds me. With my eyes closed, my breathing slows. I try to grasp for more but there is no more.

I continue to feel cold and numb. I feel weak and lethargic. I don't know where I am or what I should do. Then again, I grasp for air. But there is none. I now feel the pain. The pain deep inside me further tightens my chest. I feel confused and shaky. My thoughts will not think of anything more than what I need. My heart is now beating faster. It resonates within my chest. Slowly, my heart accepts the fate it has to be. It slows. Very slowly. Quietly I lay in the dark, cold and alone.

"There is another form of being with them," Gary suddenly blurted out, to which Mary seconded.

"Indeed, there is another form of being down there with them."

"What is it?" Tony asked.

Obviously Mary, Gary and the rest of the group within the circle are observing from the point of view of a third person while I was re-living the past from the first-person perspective, they are simply looking at the situation as spectators.

"I do not exactly know," Mary said.

"I think that this being caused the first diver to panic," Gary followed.

"Can you describe it?" Tony asked.

Nobody answered.

"Is it another form of intelligent being, an extraterrestrial?" Tony asked with a sense of urgency and certainty.

"I do not see anything," I said impatiently.

"That is because you are seeing things from the point of view of the female diver," Roselle replied. "We are trying to see it from an observer's point of view."

Perspiration dripped from my face continuously. The cave is hot and arid. The air is stale and dormant. Very audible now are the splashes of water on the rocky edges that have been toned down.

In place thereof is a bubbling sound, a sound that's very much similar to the resonance created by a diver's air bubbles as he or she surfaces.

Tony further again asked about the being from deep down under the chambers. However, none of us could elicit any more information other than what we have. The last diver must have seen the being, causing him to panic.

In his frenzy, he aggravated the situation they were in. They eventually lost the battle. During the three days that they were physically lost in the area, the beings must have taken them for whatever purpose they might have. They returned the bodies three days later.

"Will it be okay for other divers to continue diving in this place?" George asked, sounding concerned.

"No. We would like you to seal this place off so that no further harm will happen," the female said through me, her answer coming in the form of a voice from the dark.

"I do not think sealing the place will be fine. Someday, when science and technology have further been developed, man could always explore these chambers and caves for further knowledge and enlightenment. Are there any other ways we could prevent further accidents?" Tony asked.

"A memorial of sort to remind the adventures," came the reply.
"In what form?" Paul asked.

In my darkened mind, I saw the entrance to the second chamber. Just before the opening, an array of diver's equipments and oddities are neatly stacked therein. Alongside it is an epitaph, recalling the history and the grim consequences that came about to the 3 unfortunate divers.

"Is there anything more you would like us to do?" Tony inquired further.

"Take good care of a young girl who dives here. Her adventurous spirit might cause her harm. Watch over her until she is 14," the female diver said.

"Do you know anybody that she might be referring to?" Tony asked Paul and George.

"I think we do. One of our VIP guests has a 13-year old daughter who dives. She is certified and is the only adolescent diver we have at the resort," Paul said, sounding surprised.

"Say a prayer for us on the day we died," added the male diver.

"Would it be okay for us to bring in tourists and show the place off?" George inquired.

"Yes," the female diver said.

"Do you see the light?" I inquired.

"Yes we do, but we choose to stay to guard the place," the divers said.

"Thank you very much for giving us the time to converse with you. We hope that you will find peace and the light as soon as possible. We will try to let the developers of this place follow your suggestions. Again, thank you very much," Tony finally said.

Before finally breaking the circle, Tony asked the questors if an old man does exist way beyond his back towards the corner where the cave's ceiling and floor meet.

"Yes, there is an old man," Gary confirmed.

"He looks like a wizard. Very old but very powerful. His hair is long as well as his beard. He yields a staff. He is presently looking down at us," I said.

"Does he have any message?" Tony wanted to know. "Avoid the second chamber," I replied.
"Why?"

"Avoid the second chamber," the old man again said to me, and with this, we started closing the circle.

As we broke the circle, the bubbling sound disappeared and the splashing waves again took centre stage. As George offered some traditional goods to the statue of the Virgin Mary, some of the questors took time to gather a few souvenir stones.

When everyone had pocketed enough, we descended the inclined pathway back to the shallow edge towards the boats. But to our surprise, the boats were nowhere to be found.

Paul then informed us that the boats have gone out ahead of us and were waiting for us outside at the opening of the cave, out in the open sea. The boats had to be brought out soon after we have been dropped off because the water would soon rise and it would totally cover the cave's entrance.

When that happens, the boats would not be able to get out and we will all be stuck inside the cave until low tide.

"We will have to swim out of the cave," Paul gingerly informed us.

"Are you sure?" I asked.

"Don't worry. Your life vests will help keep you afloat," he affirmed.

We all worked our way out of the cavern. The water is now very cold. We swam, crawled, backstroked and even floated our way out of the 45 to 50 meter passage.

"Be careful with the corals, they're razor-sharp. Watch out also for the eel," Paul reminded us.

"Remember, in any case, GO TO THE LIGHT," Tony mischievously said.

The passage was deep and irregular. Corals were also everywhere. The cavern's small opening is now almost submerged in seawater. The boats were indeed waiting for us outside.

Under the cave's opening, we had to swim in turns, back into the safety of the open seas. As the sun was rising higher into its place above the entrance, the cave's orifice hides and withdraws back into its darkened abyss, taking with it are its dark secrets and all the mysteries it hold so dearly down in its deeper chambers.

Fortunately, we did not encounter any jellyfishes, electric eels and beings pulling at our legs. A few coral scratches on our knees were all we got.

As we neared the resort's docking pad, the gentle breeze that is blowing a few minutes ago suddenly died down. Not even the leaves of the coconut trees moved or swayed.

Barely audible in the distance was the sound of the incoming ocean tide thrashing into the mighty granite rocks of the mountainside breakwater. It slapped itself vigorously with each surge. Yet farther away from the seashores of Coral Cove, the dark and uncertain waters of the ocean conceal a less known fact of what lies beneath in its graveyard belly.

Still, even the most wary humans can not hide the fact that the mountain side also holds its very own secret and arcane dwellers of the night.

The blackness of the night, the mystical denizens of the mountain forests, and the unfathomable depths of the ocean combine to endow Coral Cove with the beauty and splendour it has always been renowned for.

Deva

Spirit Questors did not at all involve, nor concentrated on, human spirits.

Occasionally, people would call the group for a paranormal distur-bance which they falsely conclude as having been caused by human spirits. Although they are correct in presuming that these are, indeed, spirits, not all of them are human spirits however.

Other unnatural occurrences may also be caused by entities other than human origins. These are what we call elemental spirits; those that are related with the 4 known basic elements of life: Earth, Water, Fire, and Air.

As may be gleaned from their classification, these nature spirits would usually favor one over the other elements named. A water spirit favors water in the same way that an earth elemental favors the earth and all its associates.

Theoretically, these nature spirits have existed far longer than most of us. They settled ages ago before any of us humans ever did. Although they existed on a different level or plane, they were first to occupy the earth compared to us humans.

Looking back before the very first civilization evolved and developed, one can see that there was nothing in this world except nature itself. Thus, before anything else, the basic elements are already existed prior to the existence of all physical life forms.

It seems that the emergence of developed communities has some-how disquieted the otherwise peaceful existence of the nature spirits. Man's gross neglect and disrespect for 'the unseen' has brought with it some sort of displeasure and anger in some of the spirits.

As with the way people exist and how we show displeasure for certain things, the nature spirits also know how to take matters into their own hands. With their latent powers and wide range of subjugation over other forms of matter, they have unwillingly bridged the gap between our planes of existence.

Moreover, this bridging has somehow extended to the whole realm of the spirit world to that of the world of the living. And this is where this story begins.

Despite Sister Bianca's dedication to her religious affiliation, she still could not thoroughly comprehend the mysterious occurrences happening at the Academy.

Sister Bianca has been the principal and head nun of Beata Consuelo Academy for the past 5 years. Her wide understanding and various experiences have somehow broadened her religious views and beliefs. She believes in the paranormal and in the existence of other worldly entities other than the archetypal beings that she was taught in Theology class.

As part of the Academy's improvement, its directors decided to extend the academy's present set of buildings to the vacant lot within the academy. A feasibility study on the proposed 4-storey annex building is thus conducted.

After deliberations and approval, construction of the building began. To accommodate the building's architectural plans, two huge Acacia trees were cut down. Estimated by its size, the trees may roughly have been 90 years old in tree talk. It is so immense and expansive that it extends its branches in all directions, both upwards and parallel to the ground.

One of the trees leaned partially towards the academy's convent, and in the process of cutting down the tree, laborers encountered strange occurrences. The cutting saw would break down, laborers would get ill, digging machines would stop working for no reason at all, and worst of all, workers directly in charge of removing the trees would get involved in unexplained accidents; this, despite strict health and safety policies.

Among the most recent of these strange occurrences was the death of one of the workers who, prior to his death, was heard cursing the tree while he was working on it.

Upon the suggestion of the local workers themselves, Sister Bianca finally approved the idea of offering traditional chicken, rice and corn for the tree spirit. Right after the offering, the trees were removed without any further incident and difficulties.

A few days later after the trees were removed, however, the cycle of strange occurrences began taking place again. This time, those to be affected are the building masons and workers. As before, the workers would get ill for no apparent reason.

Such a phenomenon eventually slowed down the construction of the building, even almost putting it to a stop, as workers refused to work for fear for their lives. Many of these workers deliberately avoided the area where the trees originally stood.

After much financial loss and delays in the construction, the building was eventually completed. The building was blest and sanctified in the summer month prior to the building's opening that school year.

As planned and proposed, the new annex building would accommodate grade school and high school students, with the former holding classes in the lower floors, while the latter would occupy the upper floors. The ground floor served as venue for the cafeteria and local school stores. During its first year, nothing extraordinary or strange happened inside the building.

Not until the second year.

Carlo is a typical grade school student who enjoys playing during his free time. He is often seen running around the campus.

One afternoon while Carlo was playing and running up and down the first and second floor hallways of the new building, he tripped and fell. He broke his nose and was rushed to the local hospital.

When asked about the circumstances surrounding the incident, he said that he had been playing with a "small man". They were playing hide and seek when, for no apparent reason, the "small man" tripped him.
He added that as he fell down, his playmate also began to disappear and leave him.

Both parents and teachers assumed that Carlo is just imagining things. After the accident, a number of other strange occurrences happened.

Every now and then, the children would report that they see a "small man" loitering around the new building. Children's school items will go missing as well, only to reappear somewhere else.

Occasionally, the children would also complain of feeling cold and chilly before eventually getting sick. Worse, no medical explanations can be provided by the school doctors on what caused their illness. The school authorities ignored the prevailing circumstances until much later, when a night security guard reported something strange.

During the night, security guards would often record that they saw a small, midget-sized man inside the canteen and school store. As they confront him, the entity would disappear behind tables and the back room. Soon after, the guard who saw the said entity would get sick.

On other occasions, the guards would get a glimpse of a shadow moving from among the chairs and tables. Occasionally, they would also hear the clatter of bottles and the sound of chairs being dragged and moved. Upon closer inspection, however, they will find no person or employee within the area.

They reported the matter to Sister Bianca, who took a genuine interest in the said events. However, when she reported these incidents to her superiors, they did nothing to try and remedy the situation. They even showed no interest at all.

Since then, the number of these frightening events started to manifest more and more often, with each incident taking on a "more frightening twist" each day. This time, even the teachers themselves have started to personally experience such unnatural occurrences.

One late afternoon, as Mrs. Patrice, one of the school's teachers, went inside the ladies' toilet, she saw a horrible looking person looking down at her from atop the toilet partition.

Right then and there, her composure turned to panic and terror. She rushed out of the toilet and was met by her colleagues. They returned to the cubicle, only to find it empty. A spine-tingling sensation slowly crept on everybody's arms and back of the neck.

According to the school's maintenance personnel, he didn't see anyone go inside or come out of the toilet prior to seeing Mrs. Patrice running out in panic.

Later that day, upon closer inspection of the said cubicle partition, we found it impossible for anyone to be positioned comfortably at such a height. The partition is high and almost close to the ceiling. Moreover, it would be easy to know if another person is using the other cubicle.

The Academy Board of Directors paid no attention to the matter. They even dismissed the case as mere hallucinations and even psychological in nature. Meanwhile, the number of accidents among students started to increase. In practically every instance, it was reported that majority were caused by an unknown force of some kind.

By around this time, both students and their teachers would complain, almost regularly, of unexplained scratches and abrasions in their arms and neck. Precautionary measures were put in place, but such reports of scratches still steadily increased. These apparitions and sightings of the small man went on for sometime. The children were quite affected since no student would now dare go to the toilet alone.

Sister Bianca tried to persuade her superiors to give her permission to take other necessary steps. Although a wide reader of the occult and paranormal, she still did not feel comfortable doing "the necessary rituals" herself. Furthermore, her religious vocation has prohibited and restrained her from engaging in such actions.

Until one day, the unthinkable happened.

A grade-two student named Jennifer who lived just near the academy went home from school.

Before leaving the school's premises, she was seen playing around the canteen where the old Acacia tree used to be. According to those who have seen her, it looked as if she was playing with someone. She kept talking and making gestures throughout even if she was all alone.

By late afternoon, she decided to go home. As she walked home, the guards observed that she still kept making gestures as if she is being bothered by someone. As she crossed the street, Jennifer was hit by a vehicle, and died on the spot.

Within the following months, the second in this series of road mishaps occurred. Another student was hit by an oncoming vehicle. Before her death, she was seen doing a similar gesture Jennifer did while crossing the street.

The incident eventually prompted Sister Bianca to act post-haste. She could not let these disturbances go unnoticed anymore. She talked to her superiors to allow her to do something – fast. Eventually, her idea of asking the Spirit Questors to talk to the unknown was agreed on.

Together with Mitch, David E., and Nelson A., my group proceeded to the Academy where Sister Bianca had been expecting us. We've finally found the academy at around 8:30 p.m.

The academy is enclosed in high-set walls on all sides and surrounded by a lush, developing residential area. The academy's frontage actually faced the rear portion of the other building's short side. The gates are set under an arch way that opens into a spacious quadrangle.

The entire academy is rectangular in shape, with the inner portion left open to form the quadrangle. Bordered on the academy's side is its 4-storey building. Upon entering the gates, I can see the longer building on the right which serves as the High School department. To its left is another building, which serves the elementary and intermediate level departments.

The distal building directly opposite the gates is the convent and the faculty building. The academy's main entrance can be found where the two departments join on the remaining short side of the building.

We proceeded to the convent where a young nun welcomed us. She led the way to the building's second floor. The cloister is well kept and simple. It opened into a large receiving room adjacent to a moderate-sized dining room.

At the center of room is an eight-chair, rectangular table adorned with a very colorful table runner and freshly picked flowers. A huge window soon opened that dramatically showed us the whole quadrangle. As we sat down, I excused myself to go to the toilet.

While washing my hands, I readily sensed an unknown presence looking at me from the corner of the room. It is a presence to which I got the impression of a non-human being, moderately-sized and old. I excitedly left the washroom with a smile. Mitch gave me a "knowing" look, to which I replied, "It is here," to her unspoken question.

Sister Bianca insisted that we eat dinner first before proceeding to the quest. During that hearty and bountiful dinner, Sister Bianca narrated to us the history of the place.

She then enthusiastically and in detail told us about the circumstances surrounding the trees. Finally, she briefed us on some of the unnatural occurrences that have been manifesting at present within the campus.

Satisfied with her briefing, we asked her permission to wander around the place and feel the energies. As we prepared to go down from the high-ceilinged nunnery, I sensed energy of some kind moving down the stairs. It is formless and presented no threat to us.

The aide that Sister Bianca has instructed to accompany us refused to go down the dimly lit stairs alone. She waited for her other companion before we proceeded. When I asked her about it, she informed me that a shadow form was seen on the stairs twice.

As we moved through the building's hallway, I ended up in a dark and suffocating alley which branched out from the main corridor. The alley ran into a dead end.

According to Sister Bianca, the alley previously led to a rear exit in the building but ever since the high walls were constructed behind it, the exit was soon sealed and now no longer exists.

By now, the air has become stagnant and stale. Although no offensive odor permeated in the corner, 'negative' energies were collecting and developing.

I told Sister Bianca that this area could pose some problems in the future because of the darkened environment and virtual absence of sunlight and fresh air.

To help dispel the build up of negative energies, I suggested that she try placing objects that can enliven the place. She promised to remedy the problem.

As we moved through the lower ground floor of the building, we were led into the Culture and Arts room. Another form of manifestation took place here only recently.

One late afternoon, a student stayed inside this room after class. He is trying to finish an assignment. During his stay inside the room, a new teacher entered and cheerfully conversed with him.

The teacher gave him some advice and tips on a project he was doing. After awhile, the teacher left the room.

Another teacher in the next room who was also working late heard the boy conversing with someone. She cautiously approached the Culture and Arts room and found the student working on his assignment.

When she asked the lad whom he was talking to, the student informed the teacher that he was talking to the new teacher. The student began to feel icy cold when he was informed that there was no new teacher in the Academy.

He insisted that there was a new one and he even described the helpful teacher as slim, medium built with long straight hair tied with a ribbon, and had smooth-looking skin and an endearing smile.

Puzzled at first, and soon with a sense of panic starting to overwhelm her, the now terrified teacher eventually asked the student to go home while she quickly retreated to the faculty room.

When I tried to sense the room, a presence is indeed within. However, I perceived no harm or danger. The presence is exactly just as the boy had described.

During further scanning of the area, I gathered that the presence who showed herself to the student was indeed a teacher. She is earthbound because she loved her profession so much, she would not leave. She is overly concerned of the students' education and she wants to continue teaching even after her death.

We continued scanning the Academy and in the process, we found out that most of the negative energies were either in the dark corners and alleys of the buildings, or within its toilets.

We found nothing more unusual other than these negative energies and classrooms of ghostly students and elementals.

Spirit students

As we walked leisurely on the corridors of the old building, I looked at the opposite building directly facing the old building. The new building is similar in design to the old building. It was as if the new building is a mirror image of the old building. Much more, both buildings faced each other, floor for floor, room for room and corridor for corridor.

I sense something and was able to visualize, albeit vaguely, something other than the new building. I momentarily ignored the vision.

As we turned right towards the new annex building, through the short end of the rectangular edifice, my perception was heightened further. We strolled the old building feeling light and relaxed. I felt no unusual sensations or uncertainty, however, until we passed the exact location where the two buildings meet and joined.

I sensed a wall of energy of sorts. Immediately after crossing the pillar that joined the 2 buildings together, my sensation of the environment suddenly changed. Now, I feel tense and uncertain. Before crossing that area, I felt light and high. Suddenly, I feel dark and down. I could almost sense like I'm intruding into somebody else's personal territory. To validate my current sensation, I crossed back to the old building. By doing so, my initial sensations returned to how it was before. I asked Mitch to further validate the sudden change in energies.

"It's sort of a portal. Stepping through it psychically transports us to another level," she said.

"Ok," I said, while stepping back into the new building. As the rest of the group followed, Sister Bianca and the aide reported that the hairs by their arms and nape are already standing. We told them to ignore the sensation.

As we moved around the new building, I half expected to see or either sense at least two or three human spirits or elementals moving about. Based on the incidents, I could safely assume that these are caused by either of the two mentioned.

Perplexed, I did not see any humans or dwarves. I looked and entered the now darkened room by the middle most portion of the corridor on the second and third floors. Once inside, I sensed no presence except the feeling that I was looking into a massive circular space. I could see the students' and teacher's tables, but I was also able to see things at a different level.

Suddenly, a kitten purring softly and deeply appeared in the far corner of the corridor. It followed us in the new building throughout the rest of the tour. As we looked at the mini garden by the second floor going down to the first floor, the kitten slowly blended with the flowers and the lush greens then disappeared from our sight.

Down on the ground floor, Sister Bianca informed us that the canteen and the school store are where most of the nocturnal sounds could be heard and shadow forms seen. Curiously, I inquired about the base of the tree. With a detailed explanation and accompanying gesture, she told us that the base of the bigger and much older tree was located in the centre of the enclosed canteen. The base of the other tree is in the dining area by the open space.

The kitten then appeared at the canteen. It quietly and softly roamed inside the canteen as we watched and wondered at what it was doing.

After talking it over, the group decided to locate the circle of light in the open quadrangle. Much as we may have wanted to, we felt that it would be impossible to do it inside the locked canteen.

Mitch and I located the circle at the halfway point of the quadrangle. I made sure that the building is equidistant from both buildings. We gathered some chairs and placed them carefully on the newly painted lines.

In the process of locating the circle, I got particularly attracted to the Santol tree by the quadrangle's end. I don't know why but I made sure that the circle would be directly aligned to it. I then asked everybody to gather around the Santol tree and ask its nature spirit to help us with this quest.

While in a state of relaxation and stillness, I felt a sudden charge of positive energy. I felt safe and comfortable being near the Santol tree. I informed the group that the tree is a good source of positive energy.

I then asked permission from its nature spirit if we could draw energy from it during the quest. In return, I asked everybody to leave a part of themselves with the tree as a gesture of thanks and respect.

I asked the aide to turn off all the lights within illuminating range from the circle. I sat directly in front of Mitch, tonight's facilitator. David positioned himself to my right while Nelson sat on his right. We made Sister Bianca sit immediately to my left and the aide to her left. Mitch led the group into the Tower of Light.

As before, the Tower of Light serves to protect the circle and those in it from any psychic attacks. From my position within the circle, I faced the new building. As we began the circle, I had this perception that the nature spirit of the nearby Acacia tree won't converse with us primarily because of indifference.

I connected psychically with the Santol tree which is just a few meters behind me and tried to draw energy from it. I felt charged and secure in the process.

From my inner mind's vision, I could now see a stream of light cord connecting me to the tree, and from this cord I could feel the energy flowing into me. Simultaneously, I felt the change in energies in the surrounding environment.

From the familiar buildings that I saw earlier, the place suddenly took a different view. The new building's shadow intensified until I could no longer visualize it. The building's outlines diffused with the surrounding darkness.

"Call it," Mitch instructed.

In my thoughts, I formulated the words "come" while simultaneously continuing to visualize the building in front of me. While trying to focus on the building, I felt a sudden surge of energy from my left. My hairs stood and I felt electrified on the left arm. I re-focused.

From the direction of the Culture and Arts classroom, I perceived a presence slowly and gracefully approach us. After a while, I sensed that it was a female human spirit. Since she is already with us, I took the liberty to converse with her since I could feel that she is the same spirit that manifested earlier to the young boy.

Mentally, I asked for her name. Her face and entire individuality then flashed inside my mind, accompanied by the words "Claire." We then conversed with her.

Mitch asked her if she was the same discarnate who kept manifesting within the vicinity of the classrooms. "Yes," answered Claire.

"But why?" Kitchie asked with concern.

Claire's answer came in the form of picture-thought. I saw a classroom full of students. Together with the students was a beautiful lady with a long, silky black hair, deep set eyes, smooth and fair complexion. She is seated in the middle of the classroom and the students are gathered around her.

On one occasion, she lovingly hugged some of the students.

"Do you know about the light?"

"I know and I see the light, but I still have a lot of things to do," came Claire's answer in the form of thoughts.

Mitch thanked her for her effort in trying to communicate with us. She then asked Claire to refrain from showing and manifesting herself to anyone within the Academy.

"I will," promised Claire.

Before finally saying goodbye to Claire, we reminded her of the light and told her that she should not forget to go to it once all her tasks on earth have been completed.

"Thank you," she replied.

I kept my eyes closed after that short conversation with Claire. Slowly, I perceived Claire back-tracking her way to the classrooms. After a few moments, the building's dark silhouette gradually appeared. It did not come in full view and clarity but instead, a big Acacia tree concurrently appeared within the building.

The perception is similar to looking at two overlapping pictures. The Acacia's huge base is rooted deeply at the canteen's central portion. The enormous trunk is rough, its barks deeply grooved. The branches of the tree extended all the way to the building's 4th floor, stretching outwards towards all directions. Its leaves had grown thick and lushly colored in dark green.

"Come," I again said inside my mind.

From the upper 3rd of the tree's trunk, I glimpsed a figure that moved.

"Come," I repeated.

113

Then, in an instant, I saw a thin, stick-like figure at the base of the tree. By this time, the building's outlines are now hazy and blurred.

Instead, the Acacia tree's silhouette is clearly etched in my mind while the figure stood steadily in the distance. I focused my thoughts on it hoping that I could attune to it and talk.

However, as I tried to attune myself to the stick-like figure, I kept receiving another sensation from the building's upper floors. I did not push through with the attunement with the stick-figure and instead re-focused my thoughts on the disturbing presence in the upper floors.

After gaining a suitable attunement, I perceived that the figure at the upper floor of the building is the elemental that we wanted to talk to in the first place. The stick-like figure on the ground floor, I later learned, is just meant to mislead and confuse us.

To prevent any further deceit, we decided to call the nature spirit by its name. I focused on the elemental and tried to sort out its name. I received a sequence of letters which is unpronounceable. So, to be able still to talk to it personally, we called it "Apo." In general, we call elementals by this name to protect its identity and to prevent anyone from automatically attuning to it psychically.

I psychically related the elemental's unpronounceable name to this general name. In a sudden change of perception, I perceived "Apo" standing at the base of the former Acacia tree. The stick-like figure is gone.

Slowly, the figure of Apo glided towards the circle. From my closed eyes, I could see the figure moving very smoothly and vividly. From a distance, I could also discern that it has long hair-like extensions and a robe-like drape.

As it neared the circle, however, I got alarmed and was suddenly filled with terror as it slowly and clearly revealed itself.

As the figure came near me, I focused my thoughts on the blue ball of light around me. I tried to strengthen and further illuminate the blue ball.

I was now in panic mode and was practically increasing my psychic protection. I have never encountered an entity like this before.

"What is this?" I asked myself.

Slowly, the figure approached our circle. It is now behind Mitch who remarked, "is it already here?"

"Y-y-yes," I said tremblingly.

"What is it?" she asked, to which I said, "I do not know!"

"Describe it," Mitch instructed me further.

The figure is now within the circle. It is approximately about 3 feet away from me. I was shocked and could not believe what I'm seeing.

"It's non-human, it's about 4 feet and a few inches high. It has a body that looks more like a tree trunk, no curves or shape. Its skin is course and rough, is brown to black in color, and looks hard and grooved. It is similar to the bark of a tree. Its feet are very much like the roots. I do not know which is left or right," I stammered as I described the being.

It turns out that the widening of the entity by its base caused its robe-like appearance earlier.

"The entity has no face other than a shallow portion that's apart from its body. Its head is formed by the entity's upper trunk at the point of junction of the branches. The contours of the face and complexion are similar to that of the body. It looks like a very old man but is definitely not a man. The hair is made up of the twigs and leaves," I went on.

Finally gathering enough courage, I said, "I do not know what it is."

"Hmmmm," Mitch hummed. "I think I know what it is," she paused before saying, "I think it is called a Deva."

"A Deva?" I asked.

"It is a nature spirit, in this case a tree spirit," she informed the group.

"Good evening, I am Mitch. I'm a member of a small group called the Spirit Questors. We are here not to banish or evict but are here to help envision a harmonious relationship between you and those of this existence," Mitch began the round of introduction clockwise from her.

The Deva still stood in front of me. It maintained its stare and was looking intently and sharply at me. I bowed my head and tried not to think of anything other than to focus on his response.

After the last introduction was made, I looked at the Deva and waited

or it to answer. It opened its mouth and as it did, I saw that it had no tongue or any form of dental structures. The dark cavity inside its supposed mouth is completely black. However, no sound came out of it. Still, I was able to obtain some answers.

In my mind, a series of thoughts that were not mine soon developed. Mentally, the thought of "this place is ours" and later, "Home" crossed my mind. It kept on repeating and pushing itself into my thoughts.

"It says 'Home'," I said in response to our introductions. "What could it possibly mean?" I asked loudly.

"It could possibly mean that he lost a home when the trees were cut."

"Were you the one who is responsible for the visual sightings?" Mitch inquired.

The answer came in an indirect vision. In the mental picture, the Deva is at the canteen, the corridors and in the classrooms. It is wandering around leisurely.

After that vision, a thought followed depicting the place but I could not share with anyone.

"Are you the one hurting children here in school?" Mitch again asked.

"Chaos and Respect" entered my thoughts repeatedly.

Mitch explained to us that the Deva is now without a home. Before it lost its home, it lived within the immediate environment of the Acacia tree. It rejects the idea of sharing and peaceful co-existence.

It is wandering and looking around for a place to stay. In the process, it had claimed the whole new annex building as its own in place of the trees. Because of the noise, chaos and disrespect exhibited by some of the victims, it sometimes had no choice but to hurt them.

Suddenly, a chilly cold sensation overwhelmed me. My head started to feel extremely cold as it is gave me a swelling sensation. I also started to feel tingly cold inside, the hairs by my arms started standing on its ends and my nape and ears felt unusually cold and icy. I'm now having goose bumps.

From the direction of the old building, a loud and ear-piercing meowing of a cat then resounded through my mind. The high-pitch shrill purring of the cat filled the whole immaculately quiet quadrangle.

117

Then, the unexpected happened.

The purring is suddenly changed to that of a cry; a loud, monotonous cry. My arms continued to feel cold, my body hairs were still standing, and I lost my concentration for a while. I was focusing too hard on the sound that I felt scared. I opened my eyes to check if anyone from the group would suddenly decide to panic and run. Fortunately, no one did because had anyone thought about it I would have actually done so as well.

Everyone held on tightly to each others hands, making sure no one will run and disrupt the quest. The loud and sharp cry continued.

After sometime, Mitch said, "Don't mind the cat."
"Is it a cat or someone crying out loud?" I asked her, still in doubt.

"It is a cat," Mitch assured the group. Finally, she said, "Is there anything that can be done to make you change your mind and accept the people here to share the place with you?" her question directed at the Deva.

"What can be done to make up for the cutting of your tree?" Mitch further asked the Deva.

Again the answers came in the form of an image. The image slowly evolved in the darkened recesses of my mind. Without any conscious thought, the facade of the convent building unexpectedly appeared in my mind. From within the far corner, in line with the new building, a small pond slowly appeared. The pond is semi-circular in shape. The open side faced the cloister and the East walls of the academy. The pond is filled with different kinds of fish and various aquatic plants. Clean water flowed continuously in the pond.

On the far side of the pond within its borders, a small castle figure lay on top of the water. The castle-like figure is made of terracotta and wood. In addition, various plants and ferns surrounded the pond.

Elven figures of the same material surrounded the castle. As I have expected, the castle and the figurines were simple and not elaborate. A small, man-like figure stood from within the castle-like structure. Written inside one of the walls of the structure is the Deva's name. This, I took as a symbol of his ownership and dominion over the place.

"Is that all?" Mitch asked.

Another set of image appeared concurrently with the previous image. I envision a person placing a small glass filled with wine near the pond's edge. Alongside the wine is a little saucer of special rice-cake mixed with rock-salt. Together with these offerings, some incensed burned sparingly around it.

"Anything more?" Mitch again asked.

The next image is that of the dark alley-like corridors and other similar structures within the academy. The apparitions project an image of the corridors being used frequently. I also saw visions of some plants and aquariums in these areas. Clean running water, wind chimes and other objects that help bring life to these dark corners are other essentials. In my inner imagery, the effect of not taking any action regarding the matter was also shown. It communicated that it would be much better if sunlight and air are allowed to pass through it naturally.

From the dark and lonely corners of the corridors, I also saw a subtle form of unwanted energy slowly generating itself into a physical form of manifestation. Soon after timeless brewing, the energy will unleash itself, causing more trouble and disturbances.

Obviously, the Deva wanted to dissipate all negative energies that are now accumulating in these areas.

"How about the toilets, were you responsible for these?" Mitch asked.

"No," the answer comes to my mind.

By this time, I have come to understand that the Deva's means of communication with me is through images and scenarios. I came to understand that it is having a hard time adjusting and using our own language. Instead, it feels more comfortable using concepts.

The toilets again collectively appeared inside my mind, first the toilet by the short end of the old building. Here, the vision maintained a steady view. Then, slowly as if my eyes are projector lenses, the vision moved forward inside the toilet.

The view slowly panned the individual toilet cubicles. As I looked at the cubicles, a whirlwind of energy suddenly erupted from the toilet. The energy came in the form of a twister. It is black and greenish in color. As it emerged from within, it took form and shape.

After it failed to completely take shape and transform into its desired physical manifestation, the energy soon returned from where it came.

Then again, my views suddenly relocated. I now find myself standing outside the toilet of the old building. From this position, I could see children queuing and taking turns using the toilet facilities – a sort of children toilet time done on a regular basis. These will help dissipate the negative build-up of energies.

Then, as a supplemental vision in dispersing negative energies, I saw the children creatively and enthusiastically painting the toilet walls. Their joy, effervescence and enthusiasm in painting ultimately gave the walls positive energy and vibration. It charged and gave life to the otherwise negative energy generator.

"A tray of food will be offered once a week in the cafeteria. A small table will be placed approximately at the same location of the base of the former acacia tree. The tray of food will be placed on this table," I finally said.

"Who will do the offering?" Mitch inquired.

"Everyone, from the principal to the staff, until everybody has done his or her share," I answered.

"Will these requests make you change your mind and live peacefully with the others in the area?" Mitch again asked.

As before, the Deva's answer came in the form of a vision.

I stood outside one of the classrooms on the second floor. Inside the middle-most classroom, the teacher is sharing a short story with the students. Everyone sat around as she tells the story of the different nature spirits and how they relate to the environment.

The teacher also tells the students not to fear these nature spirits, as there was nothing to fear. Likewise, she tells them ways and means of showing respect to nature even while teaching them how to show their respect to human elders.

"I guess all these will make his mind change," I said.

"Do you have anything to wish for?" Mitch followed up.

Again, an image formed inside my mind. From within the academy's confines, another student will die. The student will be the last of the Deva's human offerings.

"No, do not ask anymore," I quickly and abruptly said as I cut Mitch's additional questions.

Momentarily, Kitchie stopped and focused her thoughts on the Deva.

"Okay, I now know what you mean," she said, sounding calm as if to reassure me.

The Deva still stood 3 feet in front of me. It is still waiting for us to ask questions. From the background, the cat continued to wail and send shivers done everyone's spine. The cat's high-pitched shriek sounded absolutely like a human cry. I can still feel the ice-cold sensation down my arms, ears and back of the neck.

A unique sensation of coldness crept up my legs and arms, and I saw that the surrounding area was still dark and black. Inside the darkness presented by my closed eyes, I could see the Deva still standing a few feet away from us.

Since we have already asked all that we needed to, the Deva slowly regressed back into the building. Gradually, it became distant without having moved. The Deva casually became transparent and vanished.

The gigantic shadow of the new building is now displayed in front of me, with the psychic imprint and aura of the Acacia tree still vaguely and subtly appearing superimposed on the annexed building.

"Thank you very much for talking with us tonight," I said as we started our round of thanks to Claire and the Deva as this signalled the closing of the circle.

"Claire, thank you so much for your constant care and concern for the students. We hope everybody can learn from your dedication and love for others and your profession. Go towards the light when your time comes. We also hope that you will refrain from disturbing people from this level of existence as they will surely not understand you and your intentions."

We then turned to the Deva.

"Apo, thanks for understanding the events that have just transpired. We will pass on your message to proper authorities. We will encourage them to do as you have directed to eventually give you a new place to stay. We hope that from now on, you'll refrain from showing yourself and hurting other people. Thank you for reminding us that while we do not physically see you, unseen beings still have the right to co-exist and live with us. Again, thanks so much for talking with us. Goodbye."

Maiden, Mother and Crone

"Hurry up!" Francis implored as we arrived at the airport.

"But where is Tony?" I asked.

"He is already inside the departure lounge," Francis said. "Here is your ticket." Francis then handed me a Cebu Pacific Airline ticket. We were to board flight 655 bound for Tacloban, Leyte.

We waited for our scheduled flight inside the departure lounge of the crowded, local airport. While waiting, Tony decided to smoke. Francis and I, on the other hand, thought of grabbing some snacks from the airport restaurant.

We loitered around the magazine shop for awhile, reading everything we could. Unfortunately, we found nothing that relates to the New Age or the Occult, nothing even closer to spiritualism.

Anyhow, we were able to board flight 655 at around 12:50 p.m. Since I was late checking in, I was asked to sit at the back end of the plane by the window. Luckily, DC-9 planes have ample space for aisle-seated passengers so I still had a good glimpse of the spectacular view below.

Screeech... The decreasing pressure inside my ears slightly brought me to full awareness. The plane descended smoothly onto Tacloban's local airport. The rich blue sea and the beach alongside the airport runway is simply fantastic. It reflected the efforts and utmost attention given by the local government in beautifying the place.

We queued out of the plane and leisurely walked through the tarmac and into the arrival area where Tirso and Jun were waiting to welcome us. Tirso is the trusted company driver of Robert, our agent, while Jun served as his company's liaison officer.

The 2 welcomed us on behalf of Robert, who could not make it to the airport. Instead, he waited for us at the chemical factory where we are to hold our quest.

Upon Robert's instructions, Tirso and Jun brought us to downtown Tacloban, in a fancy Chinese restaurant, to enjoy a sumptuous lunch of sea foods. Amidst growing tension due to the presence of uniformed soldiers and some armored personnel carriers marching around the city streets, we quickly finished our lunch and left the place in a huff.

Before commencing the first leg of our journey to the chemical factory, we inquired first about hand-crafted daggers and swords. We wanted to buy a few good ones for our future activities, which includes ritual magick and shamanism.

Tirso and Jun led us to a few retail shops selling these items where we bargained and canvassed until we eventually found none to our liking (or shall we say, to our budget).

Our journey to Palompon took about six hours of travel on rough roads and hilly terrains. On our way to the factory, we passed by a number of beach sites and some isolated roads. Halfway through, the sun hid itself behind the thick rain clouds. A few moments later, rain fell with torment and an ear-breaking splash.

By this time, we were already far away from the nearest town center.

The road is now slippery, muddy and wet. On the contrary, we are not on any particular road, but on a mountainside that has been flattened and cleared just to look like a road, but in fact, there really is no road.

Extending on both sides of the mud-path we traversed are huge trees of long ago. On one side of the road is a deep ravine about a hundred feet below, while above us, vines and shrubs of every kind intertwined with the towering Balete and Acacia trees.

Our journey through this dark, cold and seemingly abandoned place is easily analogous to a journey in the inner recess of the earth's bosom. Thunder and rain violently thrashed, and without remorse, the off-road truck that we were riding on.

With practically nothing to do, I tried to relax and concentrated on the quest at hand. I tried not to open my psychic senses and attune to the environment. Occasionally, however, it would just automatically open by itself so I had to think of ways to keep it shut.

Every time a lightning would strike, I would see shadows and figures hovering above us amidst the trees and our immediate surroundings. I would catch psychic flashes of otherworldly beings riding along with us on the truck and just as quickly, I would lose sight of them.

Throughout the entire trip, I felt a particular presence that had stayed with us until we reached our destination. I first sensed the presence on the left side of the truck as it sailed alongside us for a few kilometers. After probably getting tired of the routine, it jumped onto the back of the truck and just stood there holding on to the roll-bars. I did not pay much attention to it as I was trying to filter out an obvious distraction. I tried to visualize where we were going. However, I can only visualize the gate.

The site had two-gates. The first gate I saw is made of flat iron sheet and is slightly out of line. Beyond it, I could sense a collective energy form of fluctuating nature.

The second gate is further up the road. It opens to a large open space and has a much more balanced energy. It is made of flat wires inter-twined to form a patterned gate. A strong and thick hollow metal pipe acted as its support and frame. A medium-rise concrete wall bordered the plant.

In some parts of the factory, the walls stood unevenly and even tipped slightly outwards. I tried to zoom in on the main factory building from the gates but a strong energy prevented me from doing so.

Every time I focus my scanning energies at various points of the site, my energy would simply disappear as if it had just been absorbed by something.

I tried to find ways but all my efforts proved futile.

Not wanting to exhaust all my energy after that long drive from the airport, I began focusing my thoughts again on the physical world.

The rain continued to pour out its fury and wrath. From this point on, I started getting images of yet another presence other than the one that tagged along with us earlier. I must have maintained a psychic contact with the plant in such a way that the images I was now receiv-ing were somehow related to the entity that we were going to meet tonight.

"Are you getting something?" Tony asked with a hint of expectancy.

"I guess so," I said.

"Human or non-human?" was the follow-up query.

"I don't know. It looks human but I could feel that it is not human," I said, still puzzled at the vision I was getting.

"Describe it," Tony instructed.

My eyes were physically open and I knew perfectly well that I was staring blankly at the road ahead. I was also completely aware of my physical surroundings. Yet a subtler and almost hazy overcast image also began to take shape in front of me.

As some sort of second picture underneath the primary scene, I could clearly see the figure of an old lady. She is really old and bedraggled. Her hair is long and was a mix of black, white and gray. Her skin is wrinkled and sagged loosely.

The color of her eyes alternated between black and red and she wore a sort of robe over her body. As she stood ahead of the road, I could see that her feet did not touch the ground.

"Any jewellery?" came Tony's next query.

The old hag wore some sort of necklace around her neck. I'm not sure of the material of which it was made of but they looked like beads. A medallion also hung around her neck. Both the necklace and the beads were black in color – deep, dark black. Her right hand is also adorned with very little jewellery of the same black color. Other than these, very little ornament decorated her body.

We reached the factory sooner than I expected. Its gates were just as I had visualized it earlier. We entered the second gate and were led to a 2-storey staff house on the eastern side of the 6-hectare factory site.

The rain continued to fall, and this time, its intensity did not waver like it did earlier on our way to the factory.

Robert is already on the foyer of the staff house waiting for us. As we ascended the flight of stairs, I sensed no evident or exacting presence. Most of the elementals are either not interested or were simply waiting for us to make the first move.

Robert met us with passion and interest. He apologized for not being able to personally meet us at the airport to welcome us. Primarily, he had been busy arranging for our stay at the factory site. He likewise attended to the administrative needs of the plant.

From the foyer of the staff house, he led us to the main quarters. The staff house opens to a wide receiving room. A set of comfortable sofa lay by the left side of the screened door while a heavy wooden-framed mirror hung by the far wall opposite the sofa.

According to Doyet, Robert's chief engineer, this particular mirror swayed left and right one particular night as he was resting on the lobby. For no apparent reason, the mirror swayed from side to side.

There was no breeze or vibrations that could have possibly caused the mirrors to move. In his fright, he hurriedly retreated to his room down the corridor. As we entered the dimly lit staff house, I felt a cold gush of gentle breeze move towards the left corridor from the right.

Further back, the living room is separated from the dining room by a perpendicular corridor that runs the length of the entire staff house.

Robert led Tony to the right wing of the staff house. The second door on the right will be Tony's room for the night. Doyet led Francis and I to the left wing, and ushered us into our own respective rooms.

I was assigned to the first room on the right while Francis, to the first room on the left side. Dinner will also be served in a few minutes, so I took just a few moments to freshen up.

Upon entering the spacious room, I already felt some sort of transient presence within. As I laid down my backpack onto the bed, I sensed a presence exit the room through the bathroom. I started to unpack my things.

Suddenly, I sensed an increase in unearthly presence inside my room. I felt as if a lot of eyes were looking at me. I became aware of other energies inside my room other than my own. I haphazardly washed my face and arms and immediately went out of the room to meet the others in the dining hall.

As I went out of the room, I could vaguely sense the impish giggle of my unseen guests. Francis, on the other hand, came out of his room with a mischievous smile on his face. He reports that upon entering his room, he immediately sensed a female human spirit trying to charm him on.

The female spirit, according to Francis, lay sprawled on his bed, wore a lengthy nightdress, and had long hair and fair-complexioned skin. Tony, on the other hand, reported that upon entering his room, he immediately sensed a number of discarnate – humans and non-humans alike.

"I sent all my spirits to your room," Tony casually said upon seeing me on the hallway.

"Tony *naman*..." I stuttered with a sense of objection.

"You'll be the main channel tonight," he said matter-of-factly but with an impish grin on his face.

"Do you have a map of the factory site?" Tony later asked Robert as soon our dinner of native chicken and beef had been served. As Tony puts it, it was dinner "Ranchero" style.

The rain continued to pour on the now fully drenched soft earth. Soon after dinner, Doyet went into the administration building and returned with a bundle of rolled papers. As we sat on the sofa trying hard not to sleep from a full dinner and the gruelling road trip, Doyet began to unfurl the factory's blueprint.

"Okay, try to scan the whole place using this map," Tony instructed.

With the map lying open on the table, I tried hard to do as instructed.

In scanning a place or object, I usually heighten my sensitivity to the energy. In this case, I contemplated and allowed my intuition to lead the way in pointing out the location where the energy is strongest.

As I was looking over the two-dimensional map, my attention kept on wandering back to the open space near the large circular drawing on the map. Another location on the map that kept getting my attention is the open space near the staff house. The former is stronger and more intense, however.

I looked at Francis and he seems to have already finished scanning the map.

"Ok, so where do we hold the quest?" Tony asked.

Simultaneously, Francis and I both pointed at the same large circular structure. In addition, I suggested that our quest be made somewhere within the immediate vicinity of the structure noted.

It continued to rain outside, thereby delaying our quest. It is getting late but our group still had to wait for the rain to drizzle, if not stop altogether, before we could begin the quest. I closed my eyes, trying to attune myself to whatever energies I could find on the outside. In the process, I saw in my inner mind a winged lady with a wand slowly materialize out of the water.

I was perplexed at the vision since I know for sure that no body of water exists within the factory. From the water's surface, the winged lady floated slowly upwards and sprinkled dusts around the place.

She then held her wand-yielding right hand up and maintained it that way. Instantly, I knew that the rain will soon come to a stop. I opened my eyes and listened for a while.

As Doyet wrapped up his story about a young local man who was abducted a long time ago, I heard him say something about a nearby lagoon. Deep inside, I smiled and said to myself that the visions I have just received now make sense.

"The rain has stopped," Tony remarked as the rain mysteriously began to be just a light drizzle.

"There's a fairy who wants our quest to happen," I informed the group.
"But she won't be able to keep up holding the rain, so we must hurry."

With candles and a rain sheet, we all went down the plant site. From the outside, the factory looks small and vulnerable. Yet as we walked inside towards the round circular structure we've identified earlier, the mammoth framework and vast piece of land around seemed to belittle any human beings.

Slowly, Doyet led the way towards the upper structure of the chemical dowsing plant. Initially, I felt the energy heighten a little and then fade away. My body hairs momentarily stood up and my ears for a while felt cold and chilly. Eventually, the unique sensation faded away.

As I tried to attune myself to the location of the energy, I found myself looking straight at a piece of dirt adjacent to the dowsing plant.

"Over there," I said while pointing the way down the control room and into the open space.

"It this it?" Tony inquired over by the open space.

"Not yet," I said. "But, it's already beside you," Tony protested.

"Where?" I asked.

I looked around. I did not see anything but felt some sort of slight wind movement on my right arm. Then, a blurred and hazy shadow quickly passed in front of me.

"No, not here," I said strongly.

The rain stood at a standstill with the very light drizzle. Meanwhile, Francis and I continued scanning the place.

As we walked over the mound of dirt that accumulated over the years, I felt a slight tingling sensation. The sensation increased as I moved about in the place. I then closed my eyes and concentrated on the light shiver I was feeling. As I did, I instinctively felt that the small mould of dirt was somehow connected to something wet – very wet.

I then suddenly remembered Doyet's story of the lagoon. Then from out of nowhere, I heard a high-pitched bell ring. I opened my eyes and eventually saw Tony ringing his brass Angel bell.

As the sound permeated the stillness of the night, I saw a lone firefly navigate past us. It glided towards a cluster of Ipil-Ipil trees over by the end of the open space.

Francis and I hurried over to follow the firefly. As we turned around the bend towards a low lying hill by the end of the open space, we were astounded to see thousands of fireflies all on one particular tree: an Ipil-Ipil tree.

Tony placed himself nearer the cluster of fireflies and the trees. I stood directly opposite him. Francis sat on my left, Robert to my immediate left and Doyet to my far right. I then lit three blue candles, which Tony brought along, and placed it squarely on the damp and moist ground.

This is where we would do the circle of light.

I then closed my eyes and started to relax. Upon reaching my desired state of relaxation, I opened my eyes and stared blankly towards the dark interior space, within the cluster of trees.

Beyond Tony, I could see a dark shadow of an old lady, the same old lady I saw earlier. From inside the grooved cluster of trees, the old hag gave us messages pertaining to her earlier manifestations.

"This place is sacred to us. Maintain it as it is. You (Robert) are a good man. I am glad to have my kingdom in your property," the lady began.

By this time, Tony, Francis and I finally decided that the entity we were speaking to is a Crone. According to Tony, a Crone is the last phase of the moon goddess' rhythmic changes in manifestation.

The first is the Maiden, which coincides with the waxing phase of the moon. A second aspect of manifestation is the Mother, which shows up during the full moon. Then lastly, the Crone, which usually manifests during the moon's waning phase.

"Thank you very much for your compliment. You are most welcome to my property," Robert said in return.

"Don't be afraid, I am your friend. I will be your protector. I'll help you in anyway I can to ensure your success," the Crone replied.

Through Tony, the crone further informed the group that Robert would eventually receive a black gemstone. This is her friendship offering to Robert.

"Do you accept the friendship?" Tony then asked Robert.

"Yes," Robert answered precisely and with a serious intent.

Other than these simple messages of friendship and care, we received other messages from the Crone and these involved Doyet's adolescent boy and for one of us in the circle who should to take extra care of his body because that person could soon get sick.

The wind blew gently during our quest, but the candles never totally died out. Finally, before we closed the circle, the Crone decided to reveal herself to Tony and me.

"She will reveal her three aspects," Tony said eagerly.

"I could see her as the old hag behind you and from within the groove of trees," I said. I have not yet completely finished my sentence when the old hag slowly transformed into her two other aspects.

The Maiden and the Mother. I could not say anything for lack of words to describe her. The moon goddess was extremely beautiful as she revealed herself as the Maiden.

Her beauty is beyond words and one will never tire looking at her. Her aura radiates and grows every moment. It captivates the on-looker of her eminent loveliness.

"Did you see her?" Tony asked.

"U-huh. She is so beautiful," was all I could say.

After that, we left all the blue candles behind for them to burn until the fire gets fully extinguished. It would also be a part of the ritual offering for the goddess. Before we finally left, Tony instructed us to throw any silver or metallic object from ourselves into the grooves as an added offering. I threw in some coins.

Our quest for that night did not yet end for me, however.

From the magnificent sight of a thousand fireflies all gathered into one cluster of trees, we proceeded to the small lagoon that Doyet had been talking about. The lagoon was situated a few meters behind the staff house.

From the edge of the lagoon, I tried to reconcile earlier sensations that I had been receiving. Indeed, the lagoon makes a connection with the events that were happening.

As I attune myself to the psychic synchronicity of my present situation, I gathered that the lagoon was also an elemental kingdom. This is the same lagoon where the winged lady I saw earlier came from.

This kingdom is an entirely different from the kingdom of the Crone by the trees. Yet somehow, a certain bond connects both kingdoms. Their manifestations inside the staff house and from within the plant site are mainly due to jealousy between the two fairies for Roberts' attention.

Their own ill-centered energies have somehow reached the physical plain and were still manifesting itself at present. I thanked the winged lady for her support and for helping with the quest, more particularly in stopping the rain.

I got an answer in the form of a scene. One particular night, when the moon is full and bright, one of Robert's men would offer a *sampaguita* or garland. Specifically, the flower offerings should be thrown into the water. On special occasions, floating candles may also be lighted then set to float on the lagoon.

I relayed the vision to Tony and Robert, who eventually promised to do just that. Further into the night, we then proceeded to the worker's quarters.

From there, we trekked for about a few hundred meters slightly uphill towards the huge *Balete* tree that's perched on top of the hill. The lush vegetation around us covered most of our tracks. The tight and not so wide foot-path is obstructed by thick foliage of all kinds.

In some occasions, one or two of those in the group would slip and fall into the mud. With my psychic senses still open, I could see, feel, and hear hundreds of elementals around us.

Most were insistent in requesting me and Tony to talk to them. But for no apparent reason, however, we can not converse with any of them.

On at least 3 occasions, I was physically pushed when I refused to talk to one of them. One came from behind me while two others attacked me in front. Still, I maintained my decision not to converse with them.

After a few hundred meters and long minutes of psychic abuse, we've finally reached the point in the hill where we can view the huge Balete tree. A gigantic tree spirit sat casually on top of the tree. It is human-like in appearance with a large set of black eyes, dirty unshaved look, thick body hairs and bedraggled hair. It saw us and eventually asked for a cigar.

Since we didn't bring any, Robert promised to ask one of his men to place a cigar at the base of the tree on the next day. Before leaving, the tree spirit jested that along with the cigar, it would also like a can of Pepsi; a token of friendship and acceptance? Maybe.

As we prepared to move back towards the staff house, the rain started pouring harder down on us. It was getting stronger so I momentarily attuned myself to the winged-lady again.

In my mind, I saw her desperately trying to control the downfall of the heavy rains.

From the staff house balcony, Robert offered us some late night coffee and cookies. We recounted events that took place during the quests, and discussed its possible implications. I mentally thanked the winged lady for her utmost help. I told her that I'll never forget her kindness. As I was leisurely reliving and recollect the thoughts of seeing the Maiden up-close, Tony suddenly asked me to look behind me.

I saw the giant tree spirit closely looking at us so I had the scare of my life. Its face and huge eyes were placed adjacent to the balcony. It seemed as if the tree spirit was just looking at a doll-house.

"What does it want now?" I asked.

"Nothing, it was just being friendly, and it came down to listen to our conversations," Tony replied.

"All the way from the hill?" I asked, perplexed.

Tony smiled then said, "It is a tree spirit."

After having had enough coffee and cookies, I retired to my room. I took a hot refreshing shower to wash away the mud and dirt. As I lay in bed trying to get my sleep, I continued to sense the presence of other worldly beings outside my window.

I further sensed the presence of about a handful of elementals inside my room by the door. Most of them were trying to convince the others into taking the courage to come near me and ask me to talk to them. They are just being curios about our psychic abilities and just want to hang around.

A few hours have passed and I still couldn't sleep. I felt uncomfortable and unsecured with all the elementals around. I kept on moving and tossing about in my bed. Eventually, due to my constant uneasiness and inability to sleep, I instinctively got a drinking glass and half-filled it with water.

I don't know why I did this. I placed this half-filled glass of water on my bedside table. Soon after doing this, I fell asleep with the last thought being that of the beauty of the maiden, the maturity of the mother and the hidden beauty of the Crone, all within the context of a mysterious lack of knowledge of our daily world and of the world beyond our own.

The Greatest Love of all

Most famous celebrities and personalities do not usually reveal their supernatural experiences. Many have chosen to keep silent on the matter for fear of reprisal, criticism or the downfall of their careers.

Just like the Spirit Questors who have come out in the open so as to share their insights on the spirit world, only a few have earned the courage to reveal their unearthly experiences.

Strange but true, everyone has, at one point in their lives, seen an unseen friend or companion in their midst. The most common term for this unseen friend is a "guardian angel." Yet outside the context of this general definition and dictates of the present governing faith, an unseen friend could also be something else other than an angel or a guardian.

Most psychics and faith healers will reluctantly admit of an unseen friend or guardian protecting and helping them – sometimes, even using them for divine purposes, and occasionally falling in love with them. Not passionately, physically or sexually, but more often, with that of an encompassing love.

Unseen companions are usually given different names. They are not necessarily human incarnates but could just as well be elementals. Elementals are non-human entities who reside in the astral plane, co-existing with us.

One night in July 1997 while the moon was in Capricorn, Francis, Hannah and I made our way to our quest destination in Mandaluyong City.

We searched for a place whose name resembled a mysterious lower earth creature in Filipino folklore. When we found the place, we saw a stately condominium standing majestically under a dark, moonlit night.

The wall-to-wall mirror interiors of the foyer created an illusion of space and depth. Two huge carved lions stood as guards at the entrance. Imposing and watchful of every visitor, the sentinels held their post on both sides of the gate.

Our footsteps echoed through the emptied hallway. A sudden hum broke the eerie silence as the elevator carried us to the 11th floor. A chime sounded as we reached the level and the doors opened to a maze of hallways. A heavyset door is now standing in front of us.

Unit 1101 -- "This is it," I told the group.

We rang the bell. Half a minute later, the door opened and we were overwhelmed and impressed by the beauty facing us, we were not able to immediately introduce ourselves.

"Hi, I'm Denise. Are you the Spirit Questors?" the pretty lass in her early twenties, with short and preppy cut burgundy shaded hair, a very fair and fine complexion, hazel-shaped, bluish-green eyes and a gorgeous figure, broke our silence.

Denise is sporting a brightly coloured top and an equally fashionable pair of knee-length trousers. Standing around 5 feet, 11 inches tall, she somehow redefined the meaning of beauty. She was like a fairy princess straight out of a fairy book. A fairy made human.

"I have been bothered by strange things lately," she began while we settled ourselves in her over-sized settee. "And to be specific, it is not me but those around me," she added quickly. She then detailed the disturbances.

While seated in the velvety recliners and sofas, I kept sensing that somebody else was with us. The presence I felt is silently watching us from the far corner of the room, so I chose to ignore it.

Denise continued, "My friends would often come and sleepover. Most of my female friends find it relaxing and secure to sleep over here but...," she paused before cautiously looking at Francis and me. "...my male friends would encounter strange occurrences..."

"Such as..." I impatiently intervened.

Again, an uncanny sensation surrounded me. I felt a form of energy behind me sharply invading my personal space. The moment Denise looked at us, I returned her gaze steadily and it was then that I felt a sharp dull pain on my right side. I broke off my stare.

Reluctantly she continued "...such as blankets being pulled away, an occasional difficulty in breathing, being pulled off the bed when they know that they did not at all fall off the bed during the night, body pains..." Body pain! I thought to myself.

"...and worst, deep finger-like scratches on the shoulders and back," Denise finally finished.

"Interesting," was all Francis can say as he teasingly looked at me.

Ahhh. I must admit, Denise is indeed very beautiful!

By the time we were all gathered around Denise's room to start the circle of light, Francis and I have already isolated the cause of all these disturbances -- a fairy, an excessively jealous and protective type of fairy.

And as if on cue, the moment we stepped inside Denise's room, my psychic senses opened up to its full capacity.

There, standing at the far left corner of the room leading up to the door, I saw the fairy. Dressed in the oddest of clothes, he is gazing intently at Francis and me, his gaze, firm and steady.

He could similarly be described as very young looking. He had deep-set eyes, well-formed nose and rusty coloured hair. His complexion is fair and smooth. As we started the circle of light, the fairy quickly left the room, bumping into me on his way out. I felt a sudden jerk as he passed through me.

"Good evening..." we began our round of introductions and greeting. Denise is seated to my left, Hannah to my right, and Francis across from me. A single candle burned brightly in the middle.

"What do you want?" the fairy snapped back in answer to our gentle greeting.

We explained that Denise is being bothered by some unwanted disturbances, most especially towards her male friends. We paused for a few minutes hoping for a response.

When the fairy did not even say a word or two, I mentally asked for his name. A few minutes later, I saw in my inner mind, a sudden flash of a man in princely clothes. Simultaneously, his name crossed my thoughts. It came through me not spelled as before but as in a concept. Cons-tan-tine.

Ah, Constantine!

I simply knew from deep within me that Constantine was his name but I kept the name-thought to myself.

"Were you involved in any of these disturbances?" we asked. "I am just protecting her," the fairy answered back.

"Thank you for protecting her, but her daily social life is now being disturbed," we said.

We paused for a moment. However, neither Francis nor I could receive any form of thought or response. Instead, I felt a sudden surge of emotion, a pleasant emotion. In fact, it was an emotion that unmistakably made me feel secure, happy, and in love. In love!

"Do you have any feelings for her?" I asked.

"I love her," the fairy stated matter-of-factly through Francis.

I paused then looked at Hannah and Francis, hoping to get from them some suggestions on how to proceed. Somehow, Denise's admirable beauty suddenly caught my attention. Her flawless skin was just as eye-catching as her face. By now, I have become more aware of Denise's softly clasped hand in my left. I could feel it! Its softness, warmth and ... arrrggghh....

I suddenly felt a sharp but disturbing dull ache on my right side that abruptly intruded my thoughts. I felt it twice this time and now in a more throbbing manner.

Two different worlds with entirely different characteristics flashed in my mind. Materialism and limitations dominate the physical world. The spirit world, on the other hand, is a world full of boundless possibilities.

Someone from the spirit world could easily attain anything from the physical. However, it would not possibly work out right without the consent of the desired object from the physical world.

Otherwise, necessary consequences could result in a violation of the law of free will and freedom of choice. This does not only apply to the different planes of existence, but within the levels of existence as well.

"Thank you very much for your offer of love for her but your kind of love will not work out with the earthly kind of love that we have," we explained.

"She is my Queen. We love each other," came the reply.

It is now clear that Denise is the apple of his eye. He wanted no one else but her.

It was then at this point that Denise explained to us her passion for fairies. When she was still younger, she wondered about what the fairy kingdom looks like and what it feels to live there.

She entertained thoughts about the fairyland, as she got fed-up and dismayed with the way humans live. It is clearer to her now why she had always been interested in fairies.

"I will take her with me!" the fairy prince suddenly exclaimed.

Alarmed at this threat and intent, we advised Denise not to go with him. We explained to Denise that the fairy kingdom is unlike the kingdom we used to know.

For one, it doesn't exist in the physical world but rather, in another plane of existence that is completely interwoven with ours. Most fairy kingdoms are peaceful. There are only rare instances when a man's physical body is taken to the fairyland for a short visit. This is usually the case for men or women who are reported to be missing in a particular place and then suddenly, after just two or three days, he or she reappears where he or she was last seen.

More often than not, when that same person is found, he or she no longer remembers the incident. They could also exhibit a behaviour that are medically and scientifically not acceptable, and would often be diagnosed as delusional.

Since the concept of time does not exist in the other planes except in our world, a visit of just about a few minutes to fairy land could roughly equate to about a few days in our time.

There are also times when memories of the fairyland visit remains with the person, and as the person talks more about it, a human medical diagnosis of hallucination or schizophrenia is reported of the person.

In most cases, fairyland visits or abductions involve not the physical but rather the person's consciousness. The consciousness is taken away from the person's body, leaving the body physically alive but without any consciousness. The result is something science often calls "catatonic."

"Try to resist the urge to go with him," we instructed Denise.

To our surprise, she inquired, "But what if I join him?"

Everything in the physical world is magnified in the spirit world or in other planes of existence. Likewise, uncertainties do not exist. For them, concepts, ideas, emotions or thoughts are either simply a Yes or a No. For them, thoughts like "I do not know, maybe or why not," simply don't exist. Worse, such uncertainties are often interpreted in the spirit world as a resounding confirmation and affirmation.

While we were running these thoughts to Denise's mind, it was then that the unexpected happened. Denise rolled her eyes upwards. Her soft and gentle grip on me suddenly tightened. The lovely, peaceful and utterly feminine face that we saw earlier hardened. It became tense, in fact.

"Denise, Denise," we called on her as we gently started tapping on her shoulders. We got no response. "Denise," we called again.

Francis and Hannah then looked at me. We were losing her, and fast!

Had we known her inner most thoughts, we would not have let her join our circle in the first place. A mixed feeling of fear and anger surfaced in me. I was frightened of what was happening and in the thought of losing an agent in a quest.

I should have known better. On most quests, we normally exclude agents in our psychic scanning as we take them for granted. I'm the one responsible for this group. I was angry at Constantine for his self-ish motives but I also felt mad at myself at the same time.

A few moments later, I soon realized that I should not feel this way. Constantine does not fully understand our human ways of love. To a certain extent, I should be able make him learn and understand the true concept of human love.

"Let us shower Denise with unconditional love," I began instructing the group. An eerie silence soon followed. Everybody's thoughts flowed out which were all focused on Denise. She became the target of our "love beams."

"Denise," I tapped her shoulder as I called her a second time.

She soon opened her eyes, but stared blankly outside the window. Unmoving and still not responsive to us, I then squeezed her hand, gently at first until I was sure she could feel my hands holding hers.

"Denise?" I called. She looked at me unblinking and staring intently. Her grip was tight and strong, and her face looked tense and hard.

"Do you know who we are?" I asked, with the intent of knowing her true orientation of the situation.
"Yes, I do," she replied rather coldly. I was not convinced.

"We thought you have gone off with him," I said with a deep feeling of uncertainty.

"What if I do?" she monotonously replied.

"Never entertain the thought of going, okay?" I told her.

Denise continued staring back at me. Her face was tense and her feelings seemed unmoving. I stared back at her while trying to fight my inner feelings of doubt.

"What if she did like to join me?" Denise forcefully said. Denise now had a fixed stare. Only her lips moved in reply to our questions and instructions.

I tried to counter her strong grip of my hands with all my might. By this time, Denise is now staring fiercely at me. I held her hand back and forced it down as I felt it generating energy. I tried to recall her last sentence. I looked at Francis, trying to get his attention, while still carefully guarding and observing Denise.

"Francis, I have a feeling this is not Denise," I said softly.

"I think so, too," Reggie affirmed.

Denise continued staring blankly at me. The fire in her eyes was so intense I could feel its scorching presence pass through me. I stared back at Denise not wanting to break our eye contact.

It was during this few seconds of concentrated gaze at Denise that I saw the fairy, Constantine. He is long-haired and had a well-built body, a very well-formed physique. His skin was fairer than fair and was as smooth as silk. His face, devoid of any facial lines or contour common to humans, looked very intense.

"Are you thinking who I think she is?" I blurted out to the group.

"Yes, I do," Francis and Hannah chorused.

Simultaneously as if on cue, Francis and I then called out on her. "Denise, Denise, please come back," we called on her again after a few seconds while I maintained eye contact with her.

Denise is still looking fiercely at me, watching every move I make.

In a sudden fluid-like motion, Denise then threw her head back and up, closed her eyes, then trembled.

"Denise, come back. You must fight him. You shouldn't go," Francis and I alternately encouraged her. Still, she held her head back, her eyes closed.

"Let us focus all our unconditional love at her again," I instructed the group. "I want our love to be more intense this time, and so much stronger than before," I followed-up.

A long moment of silence soon followed. Clearly, in the inner eye of a well-developed psychic, a steady flow of love energy flowed from each person within the circle towards Denise. She is being showered with the individual and collective love energies of those in the circle.

"Our love should be stronger than the love being now offered by the fairy," I reminded the group.

If we were to oppose Constantine's immense fairy love for Denise, it should be a love greater than his, "for love is the greatest of all."

Our love should be greater, stronger, and more overwhelming than that which Constantine offers. Otherwise, our efforts would be futile against someone whose weapon is more powerful and stronger.

The next 3 to 4 minutes was spent on focusing our love to Denise. Having exhausted our energy, Francis and I again called out to her, "Denise, do not go. Fight it."

At this point, Denise does not respond still. Her head is still thrown back and her eyes were closed. Her eyelids twitched uncontrollably. "You can do it, fight it." I encouraged her.

Then, her strong grasp on my left hand slowly started to loosen up. Her soft and gentle touch has returned. From a heavenward tilt, her head started to limp down.

We could see that she had become very weak and tired.

"Denise," we called out to her once more. Slowly, she looked at us, her eyes, bewildered and surprised. By this time, her face has again registered a lovely looking young woman: a perfectly-formed nose, a full red-tinged lip coupled with a hazel-shaped, bluish-green eyes and her well-formed face is back. But still, she is silent.

"Do you know who we are?" I again asked, wanting to know if she is now oriented to the real situation. "Spirit Questors," she replied quite calmly but surprised.

"Where are you and what are you doing?" I again asked her.

"Here in my flat and we're doing some spirit questing," she replied.

An obvious sigh of relief is then heard from the group as it likewise registered on our faces. At last, we have the real Denise back! This is Denise. The same beautiful person we had conversed with earlier.

"Do you remember anything about what just happened?" I asked.

"No. Why? What happened?" she asked rather seriously.

"Nothing much, except that we momentarily lost you to him," I said. We wanted to save the details of the experience until after the circle of light.

"I feel weak and tired," she complained.
"Okay. Let us close the circle of light now," I said.

In closing the circle, we gave the presence within us a round of thanks for the quest. We further repeated our good intentions and hoped that everything will soon be okay.

"We thank you for this quest. We likewise thank you for protecting Denise. We would like to remind you that the kind of love you offer to Denise is of a different kind from what we have in this plane. We ask of you to instead show this love in another form, such as being her guide and protector," we intoned.

It is now Denise's turn to close the circle. It took a while for her to begin and say something.

Clearly, she had all the events, experiences and thoughts jamming her. She is trying to compose and organize her thoughts. Finally, "I know you know who I am. Thank you for offering me your thoughtfulness and love. However, we both know that this love is not going to work out. I wish these disturbances to end now. Again, thank you very much." A moment of tranquillity soon filled the air.

We deeply felt the strong emotional context of Denise's remarks. "Is there anything more you'd like to say?" I asked. "We can still be friends," Denise said. "Can you show yourself to me?"

"You have already seen me," Constantine replied.

"I don't think I remember," Denise said with a look of perplexity.

From the far corner of the room, I discerned a shadow emerge from the darkness, a shadow form that gradually surfaced from the wall.

"Denise," I began, "he is showing himself to you now. Try to feel his presence and focus clearly on it." "I can feel something towards my left. I can see a shadow form, and..." Denise soon trailed off.

We closed the circle, then ushered Denise to the living room for a debriefing with Hannah.

"Does he have a name?" Denise asked soon after.

Francis gave me a quick glance. I gave him a reassuring smile. "His name is Constantine," Francis answered.

Obviously surprised, "Oh no," she whispered.

"Why? Is there any problem?" we asked her, quite worried.

"Nothing, except that," Denise paused, "...since my early adolescent days, I've been so fascinated with that name for no apparent reason at all. I just liked that name so much." It seems that the pieces of the puzzle are now slowly fitting into place.

Denise's outlook and appearance, the unnatural disturbances, her fascination for fairy stories, and many other inanities now all seem to be interconnected.

Hannah continued to enlighten Denise about her queries. Meanwhile, Francis and I decided to go back inside the dark room to finish the quest properly. We wanted to talk to Constantine once more.

As we sat facing each other, we both descended to meditative state of consciousness. My body hairs started standing up on its roots. I felt a sudden chill around me. A chill that sent shivers down my head to my spine, back and legs. I felt very cold.

"He is here," Francis informed me.

We took turns talking to Constantine in both of our mind's eyes and thoughts. Collectively known as extra-sensory perception or ESP, I asked the questions and Francis answered for Constantine. At times, Francis would ask questions and I would answer for Constantine.
We explained to Constantine the true meaning of love among us humans. Human love is bounded by limitations and expectations. We cautiously told Constantine that his kind of love will not fully be under-

stood by any human in our plane of existence because man is physically bounded by human concepts.

Human love, at present, is a conditional kind of love. It is a kind of love that expects something in return, a selfish and egocentric form of love.

We instead suggested for him to re-focus his love for Denise in a way that can be understood by human standards. We asked him to be Denise's protector and guide in this realm. Doing so would make Denise understand his form of love no matter how out-of-this-world it might be.

Constantine thought for a while, then kept silent for a few minutes.

"Yes I will," Constantine replied through Reggie.

"I hope you will keep your promise," I confirmed his statement.

"We keep our promises. But you must also learn to keep yours and do as you have promised," he said.

I kept my silence as a form of acceptance. "You have 3 promises to fulfil," Constantine again repeated through Francis. I was surprised and simply taken aback and momentarily tongue-tied at his remark.

"You have three promises to fulfil," he again emphasized. Still bewildered, I replied, "I will keep my promises."

Indeed, I do have three unfulfilled promises. A personal promise to people that will relatively expire unfinished in three days. Yet, what surprised me the most is the fact that these promises were made only between me and the three different persons involved.

Francis smiled at me teasingly. Constantine left us without a word or thought. How could he have known my promises?

Perplexed and amused, the revelation continued to haunt me up to this day. Nevertheless, we closed the circle of light with a newfound meaning in life.

I wholeheartedly thanked Constantine for helping enlighten me on a dominant but present human trait which somehow hinders on our personal and character growth.

I was not too honest with Constantine. I had no right to reaffirm his promise with me when I myself do not stick to my own promises. I did not accept his words as much as I did not accept mine.

Indeed, man is a great pretender. I wanted Constantine to fulfil his promise but I could not do so with my own. How then can I be an example of sincerity and honesty? How can I ask others to be true when I am not true myself. Yet this experience has taught me well. I see it as a soliloquy, a change in my personal outlook in life.

Just as these quests have made me look at myself more clearly and ultimately, to change, and so did it change Denise's life. A change that is not only for the better, but a change that's for the best.

After about 3 months since our quest, Denise went on a personal journey in life to find her true self. She is now happily married, and has since possessed a much better outlook in life, a broader scope and understanding of both the physical and non-physical domain.

Denise now also understands the concept of love in a much wider perspective. She knows what the power of love can do. This love is what could eventually make her life stronger and better.

As for Constantine, he continues to exist in Denise's life, but only as a part of her memories.

Dolor

Changes for the best are sometimes short lived. Denise's experience with love is exhilarating and positive. It gave her a view no one else could have seen.

Yet for others, love is sometimes dangerous and unwarranted. For them, love is a kind of passion and sometimes, something that they believe can be forced upon someone else. Views on love can vary and oftentimes, they can cause destruction and stigma.

Dolor hails from Bacolod. Economic difficulties and the recent death of her spouse had made her move to Manila and work as household help for the Von Guttenberg family.

Needing additional help, Dolor's family paid for her sea fare from the province to Manila. Apart from financial reasons, Dolor also wanted to move away from her hometown because, she claims, of an unwanted suitor.

The 3-days and 2-nights sea trip to the national capital aboard the MV Superferry bored Dolor.

To pass the time away, she walked around the deck and galley of the ship. One early morning, she met a young man at the viewing deck. Dolor described the man as tall, medium built, neat and decent look-ing with a pair of deep blue penetrating eyes. The moment their eyes met, a sense of satisfaction and joy swept Dolor's innermost feelings. She seems to have this feeling of Déjà vu.

They exchanged smiles and eventually went on their separate ways without having at least known each other. From then on until the ferry had docked at the pier, Dolor did not see the man again.

The Von Guttenberg family lived in an upscale village in Pasig. Their 5-bedroom, 2-storey residence boasts of a large backyard with a good-sized gazebo at the far end. A bean shape swimming pool sits near the Banaba tree at the far corner.

Dolor's stay with the family had been quite peaceful, until one night, when she started to act frenzied and terrified.

She would squeeze herself under the bed, and cry. She would also lose consciousness and upon coming around, would not remember anything except that a man had been chasing her and she was literally running away from him.

"There is nobody here except us," Lyn, the eldest of the Von sisters would say to Dolor.

"That's because you can't see him," Dolor said, only to be cut short by suddenly closing her eyes again accompanied by a generalized shake and wrenching in body pain.

As it was, Dolor often had the look of trying to fight someone else or is trying to shut off some thoughts. She would again lose consciousness. A few minutes later, she awoke with a feeling of exhaustion and relief.

"What happened?" Lyn asks Dolor, worried.

"I do not know," Dolor said.

"You were saying something about a man chasing you," Lyn reminded her.

That is when Dolor started telling them this story:

> A few years back in her hometown in Bacolod, Dolor had twice been subjected to a local faith healer's ritual due to similar occurrences.
>
> Twice on every circumstance, it was revealed that a fairy is in love with her. The fairy wanted her so much.
>
> Moving out of her hometown, Dolor thought that her avid suitor would leave her alone. However, things did not work out the way she thought it would. The fairy soon followed her to Manila, and eventually got to the Von Guttenberg's residence.
>
> When asked about how the fairy looked, Dolor is not able to describe him because the fairy would always appear to her in a shadow form.
>
> Now, the fairy has followed her and is again being persistent on offering his love for her. Dolor would not accept any of it.

A quest like no other

When I arrived at the Von's place on Celery drive for a scheduled quest, I felt no threatening presence whatsoever. Mrs. Von ushered me to the living room.

A lady of manners and propriety, she is dressed simply in street smart jeans and a matching blouse that's just perfect for her slim physique and beauty.

The overly comfortable living room exuded an ambiance of vast space, freshness and tranquillity that's quite ironic of being in the city. Her minimalist settee, a narra center-piece and an oak display table are all there is to see in her spacious living room.

After welcoming us, she began re-telling the whole story. Aside from the earlier story conveyed to us, Dolor also went into a frenzied trance again recently.

"How recent?" I suddenly blurted out.

"Just after I called you to schedule a spirit quest, to this morning," narrated Mrs. Von.

"Where is Dolor? Can we talk to her?" I quickly asked.

From the servants' quarters at the far corner of the living room beyond the dining, Lyn called on Dolor to come down and meet us.

Dressed in T-shirt and a knee length skirt, Dolor was ushered into the living room to join us. She was holding a brown rosary and was unconsciously moving her fingers through each-bead.

A brown scapular also hangs prominently around her neck, her hair is pulled backwards into a pony-tail by a pair of hairclips. Dolor greeted us softly and gently. "Good evening," she barely whispered.

"Have a seat," I instructed her. "How are you?" "Fine," she smiled.

I wanted to be direct as possible since I already have an impression of what is happening to her. "He is a guy, is he not?" I asked.

"Yes," was Dolor's reply.
"Is he here?" I again asked.
"He said he will be leaving for a while because he knows you are coming," said Dolor.
"Where is he going?" I asked, to which Dolor retorted a quick, "I do not know."

Deep inside me, I did not believe that the fairy had left. I relaxed myself. I closed my eyes momentarily and felt the vibrations around me. I heightened my physical senses to a point that I could hear vehicular traffic a few blocks away. Then, there he was.

I felt a piercing look from behind me. I turned my psychic senses to the space behind me. There he is, standing outside beyond the huge glass windows.

"Try to look around and find him," I urged Dolor.

"He's not here. He's not here," Dolor repeatedly said while maintaining her gentleness and soft-spoken tone.

He is trying to deceive her, I thought.

"What happened to you this morning?" I inquired.

"I can't remember except that he said you were coming and would try to separate us," she said.

"Do you want him to go?" I asked.

"Yes," Dolor answered strongly and with intent. Dolor's eyes roamed around the place. She seemed to be looking for something. I'm sure that he is now sending her thoughts or is showing himself to Dolor. I took the chance to, "Can I talk to him?"

"He does not want to." Again she looked around.

I suddenly felt that Dolor is feeling afraid. Her fear radiated outward, physically and psychically. I can feel it strongly. Spontaneously, I projected a beam of light towards her. A psychic shield that I hope will prevent her from going into a trance.

"What is his name?" I was hoping that any decent suitor will give Dolor a name. "Michael," Dolor answered plainly.

I can feel my spine tingle, my head feels weightless and my stomach moved inside out. I was shocked and equally surprised.

Dolor couldn't have known my name as I was not introduced to her as of yet. Mrs. Von strangely looked at me, "What did you say your name was?" she asked me enigmatically.

"Michael," I reluctantly said.

Dolor gave me a surprised look. She is obviously in distress and is inwardly concerned about the revelation.

In trying to break the increasing tension, I asked Dolor if Michael the fairy is around. "No, he is not around," she flatly said.

Dolor is now trying to mislead me. Michael the fairy is still outside the window behind me. He is intently looking and observing us.

Turning to Lyn, I asked her what exactly transpired just this morning. Lyn explained in details the events as they unfolded.

"Dolor woke up early this morning. According to her fellow house-helps, she stayed in bed seemingly passing the time away while staring at the ceiling," Lyn said.

When one of the helpers urged her to get up and start the day right, she stood up and with a blank stare and inexpressive face, went straight to the backyard towards the banaba tree. Dolor said she is being called to it," she continued.

Alerted of the situation, Lyn and her grandfather tried to stop her. They urged Dolor to return to the quarters. Believing she is possessed, the old man sprinkled holy water on her. Dolor reacted impulsively and ran back to the servant's quarters. She was now hysterical and was shouting "Stop. Enough."

Inside the servant's quarters, she again ran about, terrified. Dolor was hysterical and seemed terrified of an unseen intruder.

She ran on top of the bed, around the room then crawled under the bed and ran again. Lyn and her grandfather tried to pacify her.

Then she collapsed unconsciously.

The whole household then prayed the rosary. Half an hour later, Dolor regained consciousness and again does not remember the events that took place.

She said she is tired, and Lyn even had to urge her to sleep and get some rest. A few minutes later, Dolor awoke again with a blank stare. She asked for a piece of paper and pen. Then she scribbled something on the paper. Soon after she finished her drawing, she folded it and kept it to herself. Then again, she fell unconscious.

By mid-morning, Dolor awoke and was told of what had happened to her earlier. She could not remember anything. When told about the drawing, she remembers that it was the face of Michael, the fairy, yet she could vaguely remember having drawn it.

Lyn urged Dolor to show her the drawing since nobody has seen it yet. Dolor defensively said, "He will get angry. Only I can see the drawing."

When Dolor personally saw her drawing, her face registered shock and disbelief. Perplexed and concerned, Lyn asked Dolor to tell her what seems to be the problem.

Dolor told Lyn that the face on the drawing and the person she once met on the ship are the same.

A sudden spine-tingling sensation overwhelmed Lyn. Dolor showed Lyn the drawing. A sense of coldness immediately covered Lyn. Her body hairs stood on its roots as if magnetized by a huge magnet. She felt her head expanding enormously, though not physically.

The rest of the day passed by peacefully and undisturbed.

To further illustrate the present situation, Lyn told us of the previous day's episode wherein Dolor was at her worst. She was violently mad and hysterical. The Von family had to call the village security to help pacify Dolor.

It took about four well-built security guards to subdue Dolor. Other concerned neighbors also joined in the rosary and the prayers. In her hysterics and violence, Dolor has even ripped to shreds one of the security guard's uniforms.

"I would like to see the drawing," I asked Dolor rather sternly.

Knowing the true identity and name of the elemental will give the psychic the advantage. The name itself is already a power word or mantra, just as our attention is always caught when called by our own name rather than by another.

Validating the entity I can see behind the window with that of Dolor's drawing would at least give me an idea of his intentions.

The entity I saw is far taller than 5-feet 5-inches. He is about 6-feet 6-inches and a half. His complexion is yellow-orange. His supposed beard is very short much like a few days post-shaving. His hair is curly and extends all the way down to the mid-back. It is colored in gold and yellow.

The fairy's emotion is that of persistent mood swings. He is reasonable and persistent to an extent but sees Dolor as a vulnerable candidate.

151

Dolor stood and momentarily went to the servant's quarters to retrieve the drawing.

While Dolor was gone, I talked with the Von family and asked them to help in this case. I explained that while our conscious mind rejects the idea of possession, the subconscious remains to be the major influence of the consciousness.

It is possible that Dolor's sub-conscious mind had been entertaining doubts and uncertainties about the love being offered by the fairy. Her present condition in life: widowed, alone and desperate for a chance to uplift her self and her family could somehow contribute to all these.

In the world of entities and spirits, there are no uncertainties or half-hearted decisions. "I don't know, I think so, I could do, etc." and the likes of it does not exist.

Only thoughts classified strictly as "Yes" or "No" exists. Furthermore, polarities and thoughts are greatly amplified in their world. A simple "yes" from us will reverberate as an ear piercing and resounding "yes" to them.

Figuratively speaking, a plain "no" reaches them as "no" multiplied a thousand times.

I asked the Von family to place subtle reminders all over the house. A piece of white paper and the word "No" written in bold letters and colors should be placed around the house.

I intended to subconsciously influence Dolor to reject actively the advances of the fairy. A sort of subliminal reminder. I also asked them to remind Dolor every now and then about not accepting the fairy's offers.

"Here is the drawing," Dolor gently passed the drawing to me.

Slowly, I unfolded the piece of paper torn from a notebook. It is folded into eight equal parts. Drawn in faded blue ink is the fairy's face just as I had seen him outside the window. Yet his beard is longer and his hair was shorter.

From behind the window, Michael's expression changed to resignation. His dominant emotion is that of betrayal and sadness. Dolor should not have given me the drawing, Michael mumbled.

I tried to talk to him but he stayed away from me uncommunicatively. I tried to reach him psychically but he would just not take notice of my offer of friendship.

I returned the drawing back to Dolor. I then asked Lyn to lead us to the Banaba tree. I asked Dolor to stay behind as I was afraid to trigger her uncontrolled trances, even as she begged me to join the group.

The Banaba tree is situated in the far corner of the backyard. It grew tall and is thickly covered in foliage. The trunk is huge and equally rough.

The trunk is dark brown in color. It is grooved in various depth and ways. There is something in the trunk of which bothered me. Then, Lyn asked me to take a few steps away from the tree.

That's when I saw it, deeply meshed among its grooves and roughness of the trunk was a face. A huge face. It is about 18 inches tall from the forehead to the chin and 1 foot wide from cheek to cheek. Its hairs are blended with the rest of the trunk.

"Did someone carve this out?" I asked Lyn.

"No. It just came out and we do not know how long it has been there," Lyn said. "We noticed it there only recently when the disturbances had started."

My body hairs stood again on its roots. I felt a sudden draft of icy-cold air pass.

"Are you sure?" I validated.

"Yes," Lyn confirmed strongly.

A white medium sized chicken lay at the base of the tree. Lyn informed us that it is placed there as an offering, as suggested by the local faith healer.

"Okay then," I said as we returned inside the house.

Lyn's grandfather stayed inside the house looking at us from the living room with Dolor. Upon our return to the living room, he asked us if we saw someone just go to the dark shadows behind the tree from the left. We replied that we did not see anyone.

Still, he insisted that he saw a dark and tall shadow move towards the tree. I knew it then.

I excused myself and went back to the tree. I sat on my heels on

the dark green *bermuda* grass a few steps before the tree. I sat well within the shadows and over the extending branches of the tree.

I was cradled under its mighty branches.

I slowed my breathing. I closed my eyes. I attuned myself to my immediate environment. I could feel the softness of the grass, the gentle blowing of the breeze. I could even hear the party going on a few blocks away.

In the darkness of my eyes, I tried to focus on dark shadows beyond the tree. I can feel nothing and see nothing. I moved my sight around and still could not feel any presence. Then I looked on the huge carved face on the tree trunk. I fixed my gaze on it. I closed my physical eyes and focused on the image at the trunk as it returned my gaze.

I then felt icy-cold. A coldness different from the humid night air. Then in the darkness of my mind's eye, I saw an imposing shadow emerge. It initially appeared from my right. It is tall and is wearing a cloak. His hands are folded closely to his body and he walked in a stately fashion. Gracefully, he moved towards the tree.

At the same time, I saw another dark figure emerge from the tree on my left. He is taller than the one that appeared first. He is slender yet I have the feeling that he is muscular and strong. An air of confidence radiated in him. He is very imposing in his demeanor. He walked away from the tree towards the gazebo and the pool area.

"Two entities unmindful of each other," I said to myself. "To each his own!"

I sensed that the entity moving on my right is Michael, the fairy. I felt very cold. My head seems to fill with cold air. I called him but he did not answer nor looked back.

I knew he could see and hear me. I felt his extreme sadness and emotion. I wanted to explain to him the meaning of love, in the human context. Yet I also wanted to know his concept of love.

"You must let Dolor go," I told him.

Silence.

He just stood there within the shadows, unmoving and unperturbed.

"Dolor can not love you as you want her to because her concept of love is limited by human standards," I continued. "You can not force her into your own concept if she is not ready. That is against the natural cosmic law of free will. Do you understand?" I said.

I felt like crying at this point. I know that it is not I who wants to cry but Michael the fairy. I was just picking up his emotions.

"What more can I do, you have already enlightened her?" is the fairy's answer, trying hard to hold back his emotions and tears.

In a flash, I was able to see the fairy's emotional set-up. The fairy Michael is not at all violent. He is, in fact, loving and understanding. He masks this weakness by his actions and harsh advances over Dolor.

"You must let her go so she would be happy and free. This is one aspect of human love," I said. Michael bowed his head and conspicuously tried to hide his tears away from me.

"You can be her guide and protector," I continued. "You can express your love in this manner, a manner which she will understand under human concepts."

I paused a bit, hoping that the message would sink deep within him. Michael is still within the shadows, sulking and solitary.

"Okay," Michael finally said.

I smiled. I was happy that he understood my explanations. Then, wanting to elicit a comment, I followed it up with, "Then you will no longer bother Dolor or anything or anyone which concerns her?"

A long pause.

Then, the answers came in thought form, "I will try. But give me time to slowly take back what is mine."

With that, I felt satisfied and okay. "Thank you," I said gratefully.

He did not answer.

Before I stood up, I silently told him that I could feel what he is feeling at the moment because I myself have been rejected in love a number of times.

Back inside the house, I asked Lyn to call Dolor. I was told that Dolor wanted to join me in the garden but was prevented by Mrs. Von and the old man. I told them that they did the right thing.

Dolor joined us shortly in the living room. She stared at me intently.

"Dolor," I began, "he agreed to not disturb you anymore."

Dolor was still staring at me intently. Her body was unmoving and her fingers, tense, unlike before.

"Would you like him to go?" I wanted to probe into her mind-set.

"Yes," she said gently

"Can you help me?" I again asked.
She nodded her head in affirmation.

"To begin with, give me the drawing," I said, reaching out my hand to her.

From her pocket, Dolor produced the neatly folded paper and handed it to me. "From now on," I said loudly, "he will be gone from your life," carefully emphasizing each word.

"He will not disturb you anymore. I now have his picture," I said again in a loud voice, this time emphasizing on the drawing.

"Gone. He is gone," I sternly said.

By doing so, I wanted Dolor's consciousness to grasp the real idea of rejection. I also wanted to strengthen her previous consciousness of rejection. Emphasizing these statements will help solidify the idea of rejection.

I then asked her to always reject any notion of love from him. She should verbalize it later at her room. I also told Dolor about the idea of free will. It is the philosophy that she can not be forced by Michael, the fairy, if she does not want to.

Dolor nodded in response, as a sign that she understood what I said.

I then excused her from the group and suggested that she rest for a while. I turned back to the Von family. I explained to them that there are two different entities in their backyard. They need not worry about the other one because he does not bother them in any way.

In fact, he sometimes guards and protects the place.

Michael the fairy also agreed to the resolution I offered. He will now only be Dolor's guide and protector. However, I told them that the disturbances will not all-together stop and disappear at once.

Just like any suitor who had been turned down, he would still hope for a change of heart. So, it will be up to them to help remind Dolor of rejecting him.

The occasional disturbances will gradually fade away. I also informed them that I will keep the drawing to constantly have "remote access" over Michael. To seal and acknowledge the cooperation, an offering of grains, salt and beans was placed on the tree's base.

I told them that they should likewise keep Dolor preoccupied most of the time, but not too exhaustive.

Michael's disturbances on Dolor waned down soon after the quest that night. She lived a relatively peaceful and quiet life without Michael.

Not until seven weeks, on the evening of Saturday, November 01. Lyn called me up and informed me that Dolor went into a similar frenzied trance again.

She was watching a Halloween special on television when she went into a hypnotic state. Dolor apparently remarked that she would like to be interviewed to tell them about her personal experiences. Then, her dreamlike state started simultaneously.

From where I was, I attuned to Michael's presence. I had planned to talk to him about the matter. After a few minutes of meditation and focusing, I was able to attune to him.

He informed me that this will be just for a while. He needed to say goodbye and he saw his chance. I reminded him of his word and he said that he will never forget.

I sent some protective psychic shield over to Dolor. I informed Lyn that this is only temporary. They should, however, continue to remind Dolor to reject Michael and to say no.

Since then, Dolor's life remained peaceful and quiet up until this day. No further disturbing incidents about Dolor has reached me ever since. Either Dolor is now peaceful or has been sent back to the province for personal reasons.

Either way, Dolor would have learned something in her experiences in life. Although love is the greatest of all emotions, it can also be equally destructive as well as it can heal.

Various concepts of love exist within our very own level of existence. The severity and degrees of love depend upon the purity and intent of the lover.

Michael's love is a self-serving kind at first. His end-point is his own happiness and joy -- a selfish kind of love.

But still, in the end, his love metamorphosed into a love much greater than his previous one. Learning to let go and accept the happiness of the other while sacrificing one's own happiness is a love far greater.

It is not self centered or self-seeking kind of love. It is a kind of love that may infrequently be found in the human experience.

We can learn from Dolor and Michael's love affair. Though we define human love as one of limitation and egotistic existence, can we actually accept to live through it?

A love unbound and unrestrained; a love that shares its happiness for pain and heartaches is a true kind of love. It is a love that gives itself up for others. A love that you and I can also do for others to follow.

And if Michael the fairy can do it, so why can't we?

Tree Dwellers

Just recently, I realized that going out-of-body, whether partially or fully, could actually be a unique and addicting experience. I learned this only until after a few weeks when we held that quest at the Ozone Disco.

Since most members of the Spirit Questors are either full-time students or are professionals, our group lacked the flexibility to assign members on non-weekend quests.

Sometime in August, 1997, a quest was scheduled for Nueva Vizcaya.

"Can you go?" I remember being asked then by Tony.

"I guess so. With whom?" I asked in return.

"Okay. I'm still asking around who might be available," Tony replied. "I'll keep you informed. The agent will call you," and with that, he hung up.

On that early morning, the third Friday of the month, I received a long distance call from Ethel U.

She asked me for the approximate time of arrival of the group in Nueva Vizcaya. Surprised, I asked her whatever happened to the pre-arranged transportation we've agreed upon.

"Things did not work out well. Can your group take a bus instead and we will just refund the fare?" she asked.

"I guess so. Well, in any case, the plan is leave Manila by around 2 p.m. So we will be there by about 10 p.m. Is that okay?" I replied.

"Okay," she replied. Ethel then gave me instructions as to what bus to take and where to stop and alight. After that lengthy conversation, I then called Tony to inform him of the quest's status.

"Would you still like to go?" Tony asked.

"Sure, I would. I have all the instructions I needed to reach their place," I answered.

"Okay. What time are you leaving?" he again asked.

"At about 1 p.m., latest at 3 p.m. It depends on the other questors. Who will I be going with, by the way?" I asked.

"It would... only ... be you," Tony stalled.
"What!" I said with great surprise.

"Can you still do it?" he clarified.

"We'll, I'd like to return the question to you. Can I do it alone?" I asked.

"Why, yes of course," he remarked bluntly.

"Then I'm going," I said, my voice seemed full of confidence.

"Good luck then. And don't forget to reimburse. We don't want agents to get used to it," Tony said, before quickly adding, "would you be joining us in tomorrow's regular quest?"

"I'll try to catch up," I said, then quickly followed it with another question. "Are you sure I would be able to make it as a primary channel, secondary channel, facilitator and reporter all in one?"

"Yes, you can," was the reply.

I made a few phone calls to friends and associates, letting them know my whereabouts, just in case I disappear into oblivion. I then called some bus companies to inquire and book a seat for my travel destination.

After confirming the schedule of my bus of choice, I immediately began to pack my things taking care to add a few shirts and other personal effects.

Not knowing exactly what I would be up against, I brought along a set of crystals. I have a 7-piece set given to me by Geoffrey, a crystal therapist. Each crystal represents the seven major chakras of the body.

Appropriately coloured, I liked the amethyst crystal the most, probably because it represents all the psychic senses. I also brought along with me some charged healing oils of Frankincense, Eucalyptus and the Dragon's Blood. I knew I would need them in case they ask me to do some form of healing or consecrating.

Finally, I also brought along an earth wand that Tony gave me. The wand was personally crafted for me by Tony himself using tin sheets of metal, rubber and copper strips. Inside the wand, Tony placed some crystal chips then sealed the opening with a pink Rose Quarts Crystal.

As I was travelling alone, I decided to take the 1 p.m. schedule. The bus provided me all the comforts I need for the 9-hour trip, including the traffic. With my overnight bag and the bus ticket in hand, I then boarded my bus bound for Nueva Vizcaya. Throughout the trip, I played with the violet crystal in my hand and at the same time forced myself to relax to prepare for the quest. I plan to quest an hour or so before midnight. I was a little bit anxious about the kind of quest this would be.

Tony has forgotten to tell me anything about it, except that it was a case worth questing. Thoughts played inside my mind. Can it be an elemental in love with a human, or again, a local murder case?

I finally found myself sleeping off the thought until I arrived at the place.

"OWV Restaurant and Rest Stop," the driver announced, and I got startled in my sleep.

Immediately, I woke up remembering that I had requested the driver and the conductor to inform me once we've reached the place. I was surprised even more when our bus came to a full stop then both the driver and the conductor started getting off the bus. The rest of the passengers followed suit.

It was then that I found out – OWV Restaurant is a famous bus stop and eatery along the main highway.

Located just a few kilometres after the town proper of Aritao, OWV boasts of a huge parking lot as well as air-conditioned and open-air diners. It also has a souvenir & handicraft store that is almost always full of stocks, plus a multi-purpose hall that adds further elegance and versatility to the bus stop. The restaurant, meanwhile, is located in between 2 mountains.

I immediately went straight to the person who I felt was in-charge of the place, a young lady behind the counter, who was giving instructions to the others.

I patiently waited until she was finished giving orders, introduced myself, then asked for the whereabouts of Ms. Ethel U.

"She's still in class, but she will be home very soon," I was told.

Surprised, I began to deduce that Ethel could either be a college student or a graduate student enrolled in some night class in the nearby town of Solano.

The young lady then asked if I'd like to have some dinner first, to which I gently declined. I told her that I would rather wait for Ethel. I then sat on one of the vacant tables inside the air-conditioned diner, and closed my eyes. Not because I was tired or exhausted, but because I was trying to scan the place and attune myself to it.

In the darkness of my mind, I pictured the surrounding environment: the complacent mountains, the fresh and chilly air, gigantic mountain shadow all around and the overall serenity of the place.

Most especially, I tried to savour its fresh and chilly air. I tried to scan the area for anything else that might give me a clue as to the purpose of this quest.

Silently, like an outdated motion picture, I saw elementals all around the place. Some were human-like in form, others are beastly-looking and still others are half-human, half-beasts in appearance. They are in their usual activities, moving about aimlessly. Some were chasing each other, while others are simply just observing the playful ones.

At this point, I failed to pick-up any sense of connection between them and the quest for tonight. Instead, the image of a man kept crossing my perception of the elementals. Each time I tried to set aside my insight of the man, it further pushed itself deeper into my thoughts.

Not a few minutes later, the same lady I talked to earlier approached me. With her was a much mature-looking lady. "I am Mrs. U, Ethel's mother," she began as she introduced herself.

I returned the introduction. Thoughts then ran through my mind. A sense of sadness and grief filled my inner self.

"Ethel will be home soon. What would you like for dinner?" she offered.

"Anything will do," I said, quite hesitant at first but already feeling a little hungry at that point.

"Are you alone?" she asked, quite surprised.

"Yes. The others couldn't come as they had other important matters to attend to," I said quite apologetically.

I continued fidgeting with my violet crystal. Holding the crystal was giving me the sensation of security and stability. It also made me feel grounded and stronger. It was absorbing most negative thoughts and energies that could have otherwise influenced me.

Mrs. U sat across me at the table as she gave instructions, in Ilocano, to the young lady. Ilocano is the local dialect of the region.

Steaming hot food is served soon. Through the steam, I observed Mrs. U, a middle-aged woman with deep-set eyes. Her gaze was authoritative enough to make the laziest of workers work and tremble in fear. Her voice is soft, yet firm and imposing. Her choice of words are apt yet resounding. She walks and sits smartly. All these permeated a sense of discipline and a sense of traditionalism in her.

"Ethel is here," she announced shortly.

Simultaneously, I shifted my gaze to the screened aluminium door that closed lightly as a young lady gingerly approached. Gently, she took hold of Mrs. U's right hand, then respectfully touched it to her forehead as a sign of respect.

"Sit down and join our guest," Mrs. U instructed her.

"I'll join you in short while," she said while she rushed to the handicraft and souvenir shop by the side of the diner. She was back, momentarily, and proper introductions were soon made.

Ethel, I found out later, is taking night classes at a university in the next town. She was recently married and mothers a young, healthy baby boy. Mrs. U, her mother, owns the diner while Ethel owns the handicrafts and souvenir store.

Soon after a hearty dinner of sumptuous *lutong-bahay* (home-cooked food), Ethel showed me the room where I was to sleep for the night. After a quick freshen-up, I joined them in the balcony of their modest 5-bedroom abode. The balcony is situated at the rear portion of the house.

Over by the horizon extends the mountain ranges of Sierra Madre all the way to Quezon Province. The backyard and grotto of Our Lady of Lourdes lay deserted and unmaintained beneath the balcony. Weeds and other wild flora have also grown and infested the area. A large tree stood grand by the Southeast, towards the mountain.

Joining us in the balcony were Ethel's parents, her brother John, and her sister-in-law, Alice. It is now around 10:30 p.m. I then asked them to tell me about the problem at hand, and to give me a summary of the details.

"Were you not told of anything?" Ethel asked.

"Nope", I said.

The object of the quest entirely slipped out of my mind as well as Tony's. He forgot to tell me anything about the quest. Anyhow, Ethel and her family gave me the information and what they desire from this quest.

The U family would just like to know if Samuel was still alive, and if he is not, was there any foul play involved in his death?

It seems that the family is still at a loss over Samuel's condition, whose sudden death has left Mrs. U's heart with a very big void. The motherly instincts of Mrs. U has made her search for the answers to her own set of questions regarding Samuel's death.

Deep within, she is still rejecting the thought of his death and is some-how hoping that he'd still be alive. In response to her inner most feelings, she has consulted various healers and psychics about events that transpired prior to Samuel's alleged death.

One local psychic told them that Samuel is still alive. So, with hope and desire still burning in her as a mother, she consulted a local *albu-lario* (faith healer) who said that he could not locate him.

Consulting yet another psychic, Mrs. U was then informed that Samuel is already dead. Now, after consulting a fourth healer, she is informed that Samuel is "okay and doing well."

The varying differences in "psychic readings" have confused the family so that they cold can not believe which is which. Finally in their hope of getting things to order and clearing out differences in opinion, they would like to try out the Spirit Questors.

"Where is the piece of scalp handed over by the military?" I asked. "It's all we've got of him. We buried it in the local cemetery just before town," Mrs. U tearfully recounted.

Samuel's scalp was all that had been turned over to them by the military.

Still grieving at her eldest son's loss, Mrs. U decided to bury Samuel's memory in the local town cemetery.

By doing so, Samuel will always be close to her, she reasoned. This was much to the objection of Samuel's wife, who protested that he be laid to rest in Nueva Vizcaya.

"Would you like to go there?" Ethel asked, quite reluctantly.

"Yes," I said.

Immediately after saying so, however, I psychically scanned the local cemetery for any of Samuel's psychic remnants. I found the piece of scalp in a piece of small brown box, which I sensed really had no strong energy or imprint of Samuel. Instead, other transient energies were present all over the cemetery.
"But..." I continued, "No, he is not there. We will just do it here," I finally had the courage to say.

I instructed Ethel to bring out some unused candles and the most recent picture of Samuel. I also asked her to douse all the lights of the house. Before finally switching off the last remaining light, I gathered the group together for a Tower of Light.

Slowly and explicitly, I guided the group in creating their own psychic shield. Before culminating, I also helped them through the Transformation of Fear exercises.

Ethel seated herself in front of me. Her back is towards the open balcony. Mrs. U sat to my left and Mr. U to my right. The others were seated in between. I lighted the candles while Ethel turned off the florescent lamp by the balcony.

A cold wind gently blew from the north. The lighted candle swayed its orange-yellow flame. My eyes gently and slowly adjusted to the sudden darkness. The rustling of the wind added serenity to an otherwise musical croaking of the frogs and the high pitched creak of other night creatures.

"Let us all close our eyes and vividly imagine Samuel in our darkened environ," I instructed the group.

Samuel's framed picture is positioned right in front of me. My eyes remained open as I steadily stared at its seemingly communicative eyes. As I looked "through" Samuel's picture, a very subtle smile formed on his lips. His eyes twinkled and a shadow suddenly appeared from behind Ethel, who is directly in my line of vision.

I re-focused my sight on the shadow figure behind Ethel, hoping deep within that it would be Samuel. However, as I adjusted to the sight, I noticed that it was bigger than I expected of any human spirit. Its bulky figure and towering height made me reconsider the thought of it being Samuel. Then momentarily, it showed itself to me.

Humanoid in form yet grotesquely disfigured unlike any human. I came to the conclusion that it is one of the earth elementals that abound in the area. It wants to befriend us, especially Ethel whom it has become fond of ever since.

I sent some thoughts of privacy and non-disturbance. At the same time, I mentally created a blue bubble of light around the circle. First, I projected the light to flow counter-clockwise until it returned to my receiving left. Then as the light continued to move around, I imagined the light bubble slowly growing bigger and bigger from the candle's flame.

Finally, after sometime, the blue bubble of light became big enough to engulf all of us. I then maintained this visualization. The group is now completely protected.

Meanwhile, the earth elemental respected my request for privacy. It backed off and casually walked away from us. I again re-focused my thoughts on Samuel's picture in front of me.

Primarily, I wanted to know if he is still alive and if indeed he is, where he is now. Second, I wanted to know the reason behind conflicting visions of the other psychics. Finally, I was also curious of the event(s) surrounding Samuel's death (if he has, indeed, died).

I wanted to see how things have actually happened.

From the circle of light, I can see Ethel in front of me. The candle's flame continued to sway gently with the soft and cold breeze. Occasionally, the wind would blow strong enough as if it could extinguish the flame.

At times, the flame would burn blindingly bright. The more I looked at Samuel's picture, the more the picture radiated an essence of which I can not understand. It seems alive yet not in the picture but somewhere else.

"Continue thinking of Samuel," I said.

"Does anyone see any vision aside from Samuel's face?" I asked.
"None," they all alternately said.

However, Ethel added, "I can't see anything but I feel a lot of movement behind me as if people are walking to and fro."

"My body hairs are all standing up," added Beverly, Ethel's sister-in-law.

"Don't mind them," I said sternly. I knew that aside from the elemental Ethel has attracted earlier, a lot of other transient spirits are also around us, probably attracted by the candle or by the circle of light itself.

These spirits wanted to converse or otherwise, yet the protective bubble I created previously limited their influence to those within the circle. It kept the spirits at bay and respectful of our sojourn.

I momentarily opened my eyes to again focus my thoughts on Samuel. The more I think of the spirits and the elementals, the more I get attuned to them. To break free from their focus, I opened my eyes again and then looked at Samuel's picture. This way, I could always reset my thoughts whenever I start to wander. This was also one of the reasons I needed Samuel's picture in front of me.

In resetting my thoughts, the darkness of the horizon and the pitch-black environ beyond Beverly caught my attention.

The darkness seems to invite me into its inner recesses. I can further sense that deeper into the darkness that surrounds us, an entity awaits me. The answers that I was looking for are in the dark.

An unknown presence urges me to explore the darkness. Nonetheless, I cannot see nor hear the inviting presence. Again, I focused on Samuel's picture. I tried to carefully and intensely "memorize" his face.

I wanted to visualize him so clearly that I will continue to "see" his face even after I close my eyes. In my concentration, I abruptly felt a sudden jolt from within my body. I cannot determine which part of my body the jolt came from.

The next thing I became aware of is that of slowly and gently feeling light. The sensation of gradually removing all forms of heaviness from the feet to the head came about. Slowly and distinctively, I felt my legs feel light, my torso and then my upper body. Eventually, I came to a point where I completely felt light and unattached. The sensation is identical to floating.

In my inner mind, I continued to see Samuel's face clearly. But beyond his image, darkness is all around me. Then, the unexpected happened.

In the darkened interior of my mind, Samuel's image suddenly and swiftly moved to the right farther away from me. His face trailed off as it moved. Instinctively, I followed him.

From a conscious knowledge that I was seated in a circle of light at the balcony, I gently followed the quickly vanishing face of Samuel. I floated and moved through the dark in one fluid motion. I neither felt fear nor uncertainties. The dark did not seem to hinder my movement even if I could not see my way.

I was very much aware of myself being within the circle of light. I could feel Mr. U's occasional hand twitches, the buzzing of mosquitoes in my ear and the gentle blowing of the cold wind. Simultaneously, I am also aware of what's happening to me. I'm conscious of my subtle and fluid-like motions in the dark, my sudden movement to follow Samuel's face, my feeling of security in this unknown place and my feet's capability to stretch from one base point to another point which I could no longer see.

Samuel's face completely vanished in the dark but I continued to move on in the darkness. There's no sign of life. Everything is pitch-black. My sense of direction has become useless. I could not tell which is front, which is back, my left and my right, or up and down. There is no floor to speak of, yet I did not fall, I just floated.

Occasionally, I could feel my legs still being anchored to a base point. Its capability to stretch is so enormous I couldn't explain how it was possible. Moving through the dark, I became aware of other entities.

I can strongly feel their presence despite the fact that I can not see them. I sensed some moving along with me while the others are moving against me.

Having absorbed and adjusted to my new surroundings, I began to think of Samuel once more. I wanted to refocus my thoughts and vision. In the process, the darkened surrounding suddenly adjusted to a lighter shade. I can now see shadows moving about in a relatively lighter shade of the environment, but I could not discern their faces or appearances.

The place is so spacious and the "people" are so multitudinous. Numerous beings are moving about in all directions in these vast flatlands of sort.

I'm not even sure they are people. However, I felt relaxed and secure in this new place. I didn't feel threatened. Then, from nowhere, I suddenly felt a presence calling me. I looked around.

Suddenly, everything turned pitched-black again. In the darkness, the same presence that was calling me earlier has come near me. The entity seems to be just 3 to 4 steps away. Instinctively, I moved towards it. I wasn't sure how I was able to follow it despite the darkness. I just willed myself to follow it. There were times when I would quickly see a vague shadow in front of me.

After awhile, I suddenly "felt my guide stop and point upwards." I stopped and waited. I looked up to where I felt the presence was pointing me to. Surprise overwhelmed me as I absorbed the awe-inspiring view on top of me. Distant from where I was supposedly standing is an opening clearly visible and radiant.

Inside the opening, blinding light emanated from just about everywhere. And what's so enigmatic about the opening is that no light escaped from it towards the total darkness to where I was.

A sort of boundary or limitation permeated in between the two "planes". I stood directly underneath the lighted opening yet the space between me and the opening was still dark. I could not see anything inside the chasm except for the blinding light. Then, as I readjusted and got awed to what I was seeing, Samuel's face appeared from the light.

He was looking "down" at me and is sporting a broad smile on his face. He then gave me the thumbs-up sign.

Mentally, I asked him to stop jesting around. He smiled, then I continued sending him thoughts.

"What are you doing up there? Come here and we have to talk," I said.

"*Ha-an nga mabalin*" (which means "It's not possible" in Ilocano), he said. He gestured at the light to where he is, then at the darkness around me, and then finally to the opening.

I could still feel my guide standing patiently a few feet away from me. I'm still engulfed in total darkness as much as my guide is and I could feel the presence of the other entities quietly moving around. Either they couldn't see the light, or was simply oblivious of its existence.

"Okay," I said, "then tell me everything."

He hesitated for a moment but I continued to keep my eyes on him.

I felt him glance at my guide. In return, I felt my guide nod in agreement.

"Are you sure?" he asked.
"Everything," I said firmly.

"Okay," he said as I saw him breathe in deeply.

Just like a documented black and white film, the following transcriptions played-back inside my mind.

February 01, 1997, 0615H

A twin-engine Cessna Citation jet with tail No. 1500, piloted by Captains Ricky B. and Samuel U, prepared to take-off. Its flight plan is recorded to fly to Cagayan De Oro City in Misamis Oriental.

After having conveyed the passengers which includes a high ranking government official, the plane is set to fly to Butuan City in Agusan Del Norte for refuelling before going back to Cagayan De Oro to bring the passengers to another place.

The plane arrived safely at Cagayan De Oro hours after it left Manila. Shortly thereafter, the plane took off for Butuan City. After having gone through the routine check-up and needed re-fueling, the Cessna took off for Misamis Oriental.

On its way to Cagayan De Oro, the plane developed engine and mechanical trouble to which senior pilot Captain Ricky B. tried to make-up and compensate. Being a veteran pilot, he confidently resolved the supposedly minor problem. But the problem is not minor as he initially assessed.

As the plane lost control, Captain Samuel U instinctively tried to regain power over the plane. In this stage of panic and evident malfunction of the plane, Captain Ricky B. suddenly lost consciousness. He felt a strong stabbing pain on his chest.

Captain Samuel U continued to regain control of the ill-fated Citation jet. Moments later, the plane's dangerous altitude made its final descent into the mountain of Mt. Balatukan.

At an elevation of 8,000 feet, the plane wreckage can be described as a total wreck. The plane did not make it to the appointment time of rendezvous at Cagayan De Oro City at 1530H.

Following the crash, Captain Ricky B died on the spot. Captain Samuel U was very badly injured. However, he remained slightly conscious of the event. His injuries included massive internal and external bleeding, fractures of the lower extremities, possible fracture of the vertebral column, and multiple lacerated wounds all over the body.

His scalp likewise peeled off, from the forehead to the top. A few minutes after the crash, a group of people arrived and eventually carried him off. His rescuers took him to a place where their huts are built on top of trees and on stilts. An elderly person was giving instructions.

Everyone obeyed promptly and without any question. These people were not in any way similar to the 'civilized-type' people that we know of. They seem to have a culture of their own; a system of beliefs and edification.

They placed Samuel in one of the lower huts. Three people attended to him. Instinctively, these people cared and provided Samuel the needed attention. They placed various leaves, tree saps and other indigenous objects on Samuel's wounds.

Samuel, on the other hand, knew little of what is being done to him. The pain and difficulty he is going through is so immense that he will often fall in and out of consciousness. All the time, Samuel's thoughts were focused on the event that previously transpired. The way the plane touched the ground, the way he felt immediately after the impact and the eventuality of the circumstances. He is not in any despair or fear.
The severity of injuries he sustained ultimately caught up with him. Massive loss of blood caused his system to fail. He initially went into shock due to pain and loss of blood. He felt pain on every part of his body. Every move made him suffer the stabbing pain. Even the slightest touch on his mangled body surged him the greatest pain. His breathing soon became difficult.

He felt suffocated for lack of oxygen in his body tissues. More and more blood was leaking out of his system. The body's physiologic defence mechanism cannot cope with the massive failure.

Hypovolemic shock soon took its toll. Lacking the necessary body fluids to sustain the body's needs and the extent of his injuries, Samuel soon began experiencing multi-organ failure.

Slowly, each of his vital organs started to stop functioning. Finally, Samuel's cardio-respiratory system eventually failed. His heart stopped beating.

Samuel's death was painful and full of agony. Just before his actual death, Samuel accepted the fact that he would soon die. Samuel's crossover from life to death is so fast that the instant he expired, he was over to the other side. He quickly and instantly passed the cold and dark tunnel towards the light.

Consciously, the next thought Samuel became aware of just after he expired was being in the light. He never lingered long in the dark and lonely abyss. Unlike any other spirit except for a rare few, Samuel's memory of the eternal place of darkness is vague, if not all forgotten. A mysterious force of nature acted upon Samuel's consciousness influencing his awareness of the transition.

The 'tree people' has afforded him a very decent interment. They regarded him as one of them. As their custom and tradition, they befitted him with their own rites of passage from this world -- an extraordinary ritual, an extraordinary form of love.

Finally entombed as one of them, Samuel peacefully and without regret passed on from this world into the next. He was now the captain of his soul.

His transition is smooth and uneventful. However from the other side, he saw the effects on those who love him. The very people he love and who loved him in return, refused to acknowledge the facts at hand. He is a hundred-fold worried about them more than for himself.

Slowly, the visions vanished. In place thereof appeared the familiar darkness. Then the lighted opening with Samuel peering through it. A smile etched on his face. I looked at him intently. He continued to smile back. I could feel his happiness and satisfaction. It was as if his emotions were of mine.

"Is that all?" I asked thoughtfully.

"My family cannot seem to accept the facts. They are holding me back. Candles. Three days," he said to me in broken thoughts.

Mrs. U's eyes were teary. She could not believe that Samuel is, indeed, dead. I relayed the thoughts to the U family to burn three candles for three days. Prayers included, these will help Samuel in his journey towards the light.

I was reluctant to close the circle after Samuel has conveyed the last of his messages. Deep within, I could feel that there is something more from what I've just learned. I again focused my thoughts on Samuel's picture in front of me.

I closed my eyes with his face clearly etched in my darkened surrounding. Then, I willed myself to see Samuel again. In an instant, I was under the same-lighted opening. Samuel is still there looking down at me. I looked up at him. I can still feel the guide nearby. I mentally asked him, why? Just why? I asked him for something to which I do not exactly know what I was asking for.

Samuel's facial expression changed. He is now looking more serious and worried. Then, he glanced at my guide. At the same time, I shifted my thoughts from Samuel to my guide. However, for some reason or another, I could not focus on my guide. Instead, as I looked towards the supposed place where I felt my guide was, I saw a completely different thing.

I was looking at an airplane. The plane is idly parked in the hanger. Three people dressed in complete black approached the plane stealthily. Two of the three positioned themselves on both sides of the plane and crouched low. The third one went near the plane. The third man quickly lifted a metal sheet on the plane's side and manipulated something inside it. In just a short a time, the 3 of them left as quietly as they have approached the plane.

Slowly, my guide came into focus. A silhouette-shadow of a person in robe. I can not see his face or his body. Yet his arcane presentation did not frighten me. Instead, I felt comfortable and secure with him. After a while, he bowed down and slowly, I felt myself being pulled back to where my feet were.

I again passed through the darkened and surreal plane of existence which I passed thru earlier. Everything moved so quickly. Then, the next thing I became aware of is the Circle of Light. I felt the heaviness of my body on the chair to which I was seated. I could hear the buzzing of mosquitoes in my ears. I could feel the cold dampness of the air. I could feel Mrs. U's strong grip on my left hand. I could see the light.

The light brought about by the candle's orange-red glow. I began to open my eyes and looked at Samuel's picture in front of me again. A faint smile is now etched on his face. A very faint smile.

Before long, his smile completely faded away. His presence slowly faded away from the picture. He became distant. The eyes on the large framed picture were not expressive as it was before.

The picture is now simply a piece of chemically treated paper. It is now a piece of remembrance – a memory. Samuel is now very far away. I knew and felt deep inside that he would never come back.

He is happy at where he is now. Much as I wanted to, I could not attune myself to him anymore. A stronger force is blocking my thoughts and will. In a last desperate attempt, I attuned myself to my guide instead.

I wanted him to tell me more. However, I could not psychically attune to him. Instead, new thoughts came. Thoughts that implied "A long journey. A journey each and everyone will come to pass in their own time."

I opened my eyes again. In the fainting glow of the candle that has once brightened the room, I can now see Mr. and Mrs. U, Ethel, Alice and John.

Questions were swarming on everybody's mind. I could not answer them all. I understood only so much. Yet in my heart I knew that there were far greater reasons behind such events.

Reasons and an understanding which we will only come to know once we ourselves have journeyed through this life – and to the next.

The Guardian

Going on an out-of body experience is not at all an entertaining and pleasurable experience for me. As a Spirit Questor, I try to avoid it as much as possible because of the repercussions and the risks involved.

The grand congregate quest for tonight, September 05, 1998, had been cancelled for some reasons.

Congregate quests are usually scheduled when there is an anticipated need for a large number of questors at the quest venue. Usually, the sub-circles would be located at various places inside the location.

Congregate quests are also meant for numerous presence and entities which needs to be dealt with accordingly. Since the congregate quest for the night has been cancelled, half of those present were sent to a place in Quezon City for the quest. Those who remained were assigned to read oracles and give psychic consultations to personal guests and friends.

Seven of fourteen questors, myself included, were assigned to a quest in Quezon City. Of the seven, two came from the Mages of the Dawn group while the remaining five from the Luna Y Sol sub-group. Five other non-questors were also allowed to join the quest that tonight as part of their month-long documentary project for a University.

We left the Communications Department at around 9:30 in the evening. After going through the traffic along Balara Avenue, the rest of the trip to the agent's residence was relatively short.

We would enter a private estate, only to exit and enter again in another subdivision. After a few turns, we stopped in a relatively petite house situated near the corner of two streets. I did not immediately disembark from Danielle's car primarily because I did a short but extensive psychic shield on myself. I do not know why I did it but I just felt like doing it at the time.

Firstly, I imagined a golden ball of light. Instead of using the regular blue light, gold instinctively struck me with impact that I preferred it over blue. I kept the golden ball around me, small and compact but thick enough to withstand any possible psychic attack. Finally, before getting off the car, I caught a glimpse of the Mango Tree at the inside corner of the perimeter of the house.

I saw about three huge shadows amidst the tree's own shadows. I further sensed that of the three, one relatively leads the other two and the rest of the elementals within the immediate surroundings. I'm not sure, however, if the presence I felt in the Mango tree is the common *Tikbalang* or *Kapre*. As we prepared to enter Wilma's house, the group decided to do a short Tower of Light. Chris, a graduate of Tony's magick class, led the group in the short but precise Tower of Light exercise.

Once inside, we asked Wilma, our agent, to briefly share with us her scary experiences. Wilma is an entrepreneur. Together with her Russian husband, they've successfully established a trading business in Quezon City.

According to Wilma, their paranormal experiences started a few months back. She did not actually experience these phenomena but everybody in the house did.

On one occasion, her elder household help was strangled while she had her siesta in the rear basement. Upon further inquiry from the household help, she informed Wilma that all she did before sleeping is to look at the odd makeshift room beside the maids' quarters.

Initially, she heard a faint mumble and movement of things from inside the room which prompted her to take a look. Finding nothing inside it, she returned to her room to rest. Soon after, she felt something take hold of her neck. She tried to breath but the pressure on her throat was suffocating. She started to feel short of breath. In her struggle with the unseen force, she started to feel terribly frightened.

Despite her fright, she still managed to stand and eventually run to the kitchen where she felt better. On another occasion, Wilma reports that an unseen hand had pushed her mother from behind. The elderly woman fell down but luckily sustained only minor injuries. She also recounts that her mother once reported having heard a whisper of some kind while relaxing in the bedroom.

Her children would also trip and fall frequently for no apparent reason at all. As reported by the children, they felt as if someone had pushed them from behind.

At first, Wilma dismissed the prevailing problem and attributed it to her children's pure imagination. Not until one afternoon, when she herself had personally experienced the unseen world.

Wilma was resting in the living room couch, fully awake, when she felt a presence near her. She first ignored the sensation. Ultimately however, she heard a very faint voice. Puzzled, she strained her ear to hear more clearly. As she did her body hairs stood, her head swelled in sensation and a chilly cold sensation crept from her head down her body.

"Good evening. I'm here..." echoed a soft and melodious voice in her ear.

Wilma is so sure that she was awake at that time. She moved her feet and she could distinctively feel it move. She tried to shout but then no voice or sound would come out of her mouth. Her fright has overwhelmed her.

She got so terrified by the situation and of what is happening that all she could do was close her eyes and pray the rosary.

Carla, Wilma's business associate and closest friend heard of her problem. She volunteered to get in touch with our group and to eventually seek our advice what to do with the present situation.

From the porch, I sat directly facing the Mango tree. While we were being briefed by Wilma, I saw one of the three tree-dwelling spirits go down from the upper branches. It was short, hairy, stooped, muscular, very brown complexioned and wide-mouthed.

From behind, it gingerly approached Portia, one of the members of the Luna Y Sol sub-group, and tried to imitate her every movement. It also became curious of the video cam on the table and tried looking through its viewing piece.

From Portia, it went around the group snooping at everybody's left side, more particularly at the area of the neck and ears. It was as if it is looking for something and is using its sense of smell.

From the porch, it went directly towards the garage.

As per our routine, we asked for Wilma's permission to move around the place to locate any particular cold spot. A cold spot is a place inside the property wherein unwanted energies abound and concentrate. This is what we usually look for when doing a psychic scan.

Initially, Wilma led us to the outer basement where the maids' quarter is located. While slowly traversing the slippery and rather dark hall way to the basement, I felt an energy rush up towards me. As I stepped into the open-air basement, the small room at the left most corner attracted me.

It was the only room without lights and possibly functions only as store room. I cautiously approached the room with Danielle, the other member of the Mages of the Dawn. She had been with the Spirit Questors for quite some time now and is presently training as a Mage.

Since a kiddie bike and a wheel chair obstructed our way, Danielle and I first satisfied ourselves with just peeking inside the room. Then all of a sudden, we both heard a scrapping noise and subtle movements inside.

"Hmmm!" Danielle mused.

"Rats? Cats? External sources of noise?" I blurted out to Danielle as we looked at each other.

"Impossible," she answered.

Not having satisfied myself, I slowly removed the kiddie bike and the wheel chair from the entrance of the room. I then entered its darkened interiors. My arms suddenly felt cold. I felt my head swell and a very cold sensation slowly moved up my spine. As I went deeper inside, I had this funny sensation that I was stepping into another place. The darker it gets, the more I felt pressurized as if I was inside a chamber.

I stayed inside for quite some time, familiarizing myself with the unique sensation. Then I went out. Connie, a debonair young lady who became involved with spirit questing after finding out that she had an elemental attached to her then accompanied me as we continued to move about in the basement. We found nothing more extraordinary. We then retreated up to the main house and tried to go around the place again.

All the rooms were relatively okay, with no resident energies inside. When we entered the middle most room, however, a surge of energy spewed out as we entered.

On Connie's perception, the painting that hung prominently inside caused it. I felt otherwise, however. I could feel the painting's outpour of energy but I could also feel as if the whole room was energized and the source is not from inside this room.

Finally, we were led to the inner basement. A small spiral stairwell descends down to the lower chamber of the house. Danielle suggested that the lights remain close.

As it was, I cautiously groped my way down the very narrow spiral stairway. Danielle followed me together with the rest of the group.

179

"Wow. This place is heavy," I could hardly say under the immense cold that I felt. I started to shiver and instinctively rubbed my arms with my hands.

"This is the worst," one of the questors remarked.

The inner basement is rectangular in shape. It was squared and had no windows. Adjacent to the far wall is a glass wall that looks out to the outer basement. The walls were not painted but were plainly cemented and smoothened out.

At present, the inner basement serves as the store room for the trading supplies which our agent deals with. Most of the Spirit Questors moved about. Finally, we decided to go up and discuss our findings together.

"Where are we questing?" asked Ian, one of the two Mages who joined this quest and was assigned facilitator for the night.

"I want to have two simultaneous circles. One at each basement," I said.

"One circle at the inner basement," Connie followed-up.

"Okay," I said in agreement.

We all then proceeded to the inner basement. Prior to our descent to the room, I overheard Rochelle, one of our student companions, complaining of a terrible headache.

I had the gut feeling that she is now being overwhelmed by the energy present so I gave her my clear quartz and red obsidian crystals for her to use as a magnetizer. I told her to play with it, thinking of it as a magnet for energies.

I also gave Portia a crystal which I've borrowed from Chris. For the rest of the student group, I decided to lend Jello and Bibeth a black obsidian that I borrowed from both Connie and Danielle. Ian then asked Wilma to bring the candles. As we all piled down the narrow spiral stairwell, I psychically reinforced the golden light which I've created earlier. Then, I instructed Wilma to ask her maids to turn off all the lights in the house.

Now, the only light came from the single 100 watts bulb which illuminated the entire inner basement. Strewn across the floor were toys of various shapes and sizes. The strange thing about it is that when we first went into the inner basement, we did not stumble across any of these toys while in the dark.

But the strangest thing of all is this: why is the inner basement now strewn with children's toys when it should be a store room for trading supplies? Furthermore I had a strange feeling inside me that says that these toys were not what they obviously appear to be.

From an initial perception that we will not need any candles, I instructed Danielle to light three candles outside the basement. I specifically asked her to position the candles in such a way that the candles would be in a triangular position. The base should point outwards while the tip should point to the inner basement. After doing so I assisted Ian in positioning everybody within the circle.

Ian sat in front of me with Connie slightly to my right, Tracey and Lucy were opposite each other and positioned perpendicular to me, Danielle is on my left and Chris is on my right. All non-questors were positioned in between each Questors.

Connie positioned the candles in a triangular formation. However, I felt very uncomfortable with the set up of the circle and the candles. I tried to relax for a while then repositioned all the candles in such a way that the base points towards the wall and away from me while the apex points at me.

I also adjusted the location of candles at the inner basement so it would directly align with all the candles in the outer basement.

In effect, the apexes of the two sets of candles were pointed directly at each other, with me at the centre. And only after doing so did I feel much relaxed. We then turned the lights off. Darkness.

Darkness now surrounds us. Only the lighted candles gave us some light. Shadows fell on every perceptible wall and at every angle. The flicker of the red-orange flame of the candles has brought us the security that we needed.

"Is it here?" Ian asked.

"I do not have it, it is with Connie," I said.

"Connie?" Ian inquired.

"Okay. It's with me," Connie replied.

"Does it have a name?" Ian again asked.

"Yes but I cannot figure out the name," came the reply.

We did a round of introductions and verbally stated our intentions for the quest. At this point, everybody else is talking and had something to say. I blocked everybody off and tried to focus my thoughts on the unknown energy that was amongst us.

I then saw it. The presence is standing by the corner when I first saw it. It physically resembles a male but deep inside, I know that it does not have any particular gender.

The next time I saw the presence, it was moving around the circle and is having fun giving thoughts and ideas to each and every individual in the circle.

Occasionally, it would tease and do slight physical manifestations but only for the fun of it. Interestingly, he never did touch or attempt any contact, psychically or otherwise.

"Danielle, I think you have a name," I finally said.

"I am getting a name to the effect that it sounds like Dumko," he said.

"Channels, open," Ian instructed.

"Can anyone describe the entity?" I asked.

"I am seeing an arrow and it is pointing downward," Connie said.

"I think the entity is laughing." "Somebody is at my back. Can any-one tell me who it is?" blurted out some of the non-questors in our group.

"Yes, I think it is him," Connie confirmed.

Everybody else is saying whatever comes into his or her mind. Danielle remained silent and appears to be concentrating. Though I still had my eyes closed, I was fully aware of the proceedings of the circle.

To fully understand what was happening, I went into alpha level and attuned to the energy. I again saw him laugh aloud with all glee and glamour. He was moving around the circle and is trying to influence everybody into chaos.

One thing that puzzled me was his constant distance from me. He never came close to getting past Danielle and Lucy. It was clear to me now that he was just playing around.

"Any intentions?" Ian asked.

"I'm not getting any intentions," Connie said.

"So do I," seconded Tracey.

With Ian's permission I co-facilitated with him since everybody is already getting confused and deceived.

"Nobody speaks without being asked," I said. "Danielle, what are you getting?"

I again ascended to alpha level and attuned myself to the energy. I had my head bowed down to further help me in concentrating. As I was attuning myself, the blackness in my mind suddenly turned into gray.

The gray coloured environment then took a two-dimensional view. I saw the floor where we were seating. I saw the solid walls and ceilings. As I continued to attune myself, the supposedly solid gray floor turned into a three-dimensional transparent floor. Underneath the floor lay a very deep abyss.

A tunnel that leads down. As I backed down a little, I came to visualize that the whole basement was on top of a deep tunnel. The only partition that separated us from the deep tunnel is a 'glass floor'.

"It looks like...." Don paused and continued, "...the floor is hollow."

"Yeah you are right," I said.

The presence that I earlier saw is now sitting in the corner. It is not as hilarious and jolly as it was before.

"Connie and everybody else," I commanded, "no one will go into trance. If you do, you might just be pulled into the abyss," I warned the group as I saw a premonition of what might happen.

Likewise, anyone who gets overwhelmed with fear and panic will have a chance to be pulled in.

"I am going to see what and where this leads to," I finally said.

I then fully attuned myself to the now familiar shades of gray black darkness. Before going any further, I tried to describe the presence that was with us since the beginning. I went close to him in his cosy little corner.

His skin is very dark brown as if he was sunburned and toasted, well done. His head was cleanly shaven and he had ears that folded down and protruded forward. His eyes are black and the arrow pointing down that Connie saw earlier is actually his tail, with a tip that looks like an arrow. He holds a big stick on his right hand and uses it occasionally to poke at those in the circle. The place where we are now sitting is on top of the tunnel.

We were sitting at a transparent glass-like surface. I then visualized the golden light around me. I solidified the ball to make it look metallic in a sense. From that corner, I slowly slid into the tunnel.

The tunnel is very cold and silent. Once inside the tunnel, I completely forgot about the physical world. I felt as if I was at a completely different place. The tunnel is ribbed in a circular manner. Ample light illuminated the place. Not too dark, not too bright.

Further down, the tunnel curved to the right. The tunnel is now getting smaller and smaller. The place is colder than before and I was starting to shiver in cold. The tunnel is still ribbed along the edge and inner surface. I continued down through the tunnel inside my protective bubble. The further down I went, the smaller the tunnel became.

Then, the tunnel suddenly opened into a vast cavern. The cavern is so enormous that it belittled my presence. The end of the tunnel terminated precisely at the top of the cavern roof. Inside the subterranean passage, rocks of all sizes and shapes projected out. The rocks are jagged and razor-sharp.

Light illuminated the rock from within, but the rocks are coloured black and looked solid. I sense the presence of a number of other entities inside the massive chamber but I could not actually see them.

The familiar sensation of a hundred pair of eyes looking at me is evident. I moved around the cavern. At the far side of the semi-circular edifice, I saw a chair. The royal chair is made of an unknown material.

From it protruded sharp and other rough and uneven objects. The chair had a high backrest with an extensive and projecting headpiece that one would not even think of sitting on it. Alongside the throne, other small chairs of the same masterpiece and quality lined the sides.

"Get out," I heard a voice say.

Before finally getting out, I chanced upon a smaller opening on one side of the cave. It was much darker and colder than where I was.

"Mike, don't go," I heard a voice from somewhere.

From the entrance of the much smaller tunnel, I slowly drifted back to the main tunnel from where I started. Slowly, I regressed back upward. I am now starting to feel heavy and warm. I then became more aware of my physical body.

I could feel Wilma and Carla's grasp of my hand. I could feel the weight exerted on my crossed legs and buttocks. The tunnel is now getting larger and larger. I could see the ribbed surface of the tunnel as I pass by. The guardian of the tunnel meets me with a grin and lets me pass without any difficulty or hindrance.

As I passed by, I vaguely saw a mango tree by the edge of the tunnel. I was disturbed by the symbolic meaning of the tree until much later when Connie and Chris advised me of the similarity of our visions. The partial solution to the problem beseeching the family lies in the Mango tree.

As I see it, the elementals I saw earlier can probably be the helping hand needed in counter-acting on the guardian. Once Wilma gains the trust and confidence of the elementals in the tree, she will have all the elementals within her backyard as supporters.

Furthermore, Wilma needs to disrupt the psychic structure that was built and created at the inner basement of the house by inadvertent misuse and the lack of attention for it. Either she opens up the place for use, or she restructures it.

I maintained my eyes closed for the meantime. A new set of perception then surfaced inside my mind. I saw toys littered around the basement and further sensed that it was meant to disturb and mean another thing.

From the inner recesses of my mind, I attuned myself to the intentions of the guardian in littering the toys. I then saw him laugh. I tried to probe deeper into his thoughts and emotions to which I gathered that these toys are symbolic of what we were doing right now.

Since there is no issue to talk about, he intentionally placed these astral diversions for his own little fun.

"Ian, close the circle!" I immediately instructed him.

With that, Ian started to close the circle of light counter-clockwise from him. I wanted to close the circle primarily because of the ill intentions that the circle is trapped into doing and because of the negative effects it has on those within. It is draining our energies and will put us all in trouble if we went on.

The entity Dumko is as deceiving and cunning as the place from where he came from. He tried to cheat people in the house into believing that he is a friend. He even went to the extent of wooing Wilma – but to the wrong effect. It frightened her out of her wits instead.

As an initial step in gaining the trust of the elementals, I asked Wilma to share a drink and offer a piece of cake with the elemental by deliberately spilling the juice and food at the foot of the tree. Immediately after doing so, Wilma reported to suddenly feeling heavy and warm all-over.

I advised her that it is the elementals' way of saying thank you for the offering and is a good sign of their possible acceptance of the proposed friendship. It is a transfer of positive energy from the elementals to her.

It is now early morning. We parted ways with Wilma. She is now more relaxed and calmer. After having answered most of her questions and inquiries, we finally wished her luck.

It is in this line that we should try to keep in mind that people we meet each day in our lives could be as deceiving and deceitful as Dumko.

We should therefore take the necessary precautions to genuinely realize first the intentions of strangers and friends alike. Only then can we really understand the deeper meaning of life.

As you and I journey through life, let us learn as much as we can, for you and I are just travellers in this journey called life.

About the Author:

Michael Duque joined the Spirit Questors in 1997 first as an observer then as an apprentice. Under the guidance of his mentor and SQ Founder Tony Perez, he developed his latent abilities until he became proficient in their use and application.

Michael's early involvement with the SQ involved being the group's quest reporter, official records keeper, co-trainer, website coordinator, and eventually senior facilitator & member.

As well as being a member of the SQ, Michael is also a second-degree member of the former Luna Y Sol coven and workshop coordinator for the former SQ sub-group Brothers of the Peach Garden.

His previous work involves co-authoring Stories of the Moon: More Adventures of the Spirit Questors (Anvil Publishing, 2001) with Tony Perez and Dion Fernandez of which he wrote three-chapters. He also wrote the Little Green Book: A Nurse's Pocket Reference (2005) for the use of the Philippine Nurses Association of the UK (PNA UK) and its members.

Michael currently works as a registered nurse in the United Kingdom and is also a freelance journalist and news & media affairs correspondent, entrepreneur, community newspaper editor, community leader, charity fund raiser and an exhibited photo-hobbyist. He has also founded and co-founded a number of organizations and groups of which have all been locally and internationally recognized and accredited.

When not otherwise busy, Michael spends quality time with his wife and three children on top of his charitable activities of being a Master Mason of the United Grand Lodge of England.